China on the World Stage

FOREIGN
AFFAIRS

Contents

Foreword by
James F. Hoge, Jr.

The post–Cold War era has been marked by the emergence of economic globalization, the shift of wealth from West to East and the attraction in developing countries of authoritarian politics and state capitalism. These trends and the profound transformation they are fostering are most evident in Asia. At the center of the Asian transformation is China, which is rapidly resuming its historic position as a great power and major cultural center. For the most part, rising Asian countries are peacefully competing and, where advantageous, cooperating in their drive for prosperity and prominence. But history illustrates that great power shifts in the international order often incite conflicts. Professor G. John Ikenberry is sanguine about integrating China into the contemporary international order. It is "fundamentally different from those that past rising states confronted." This Western-centered system is "open, integrated and rule-based with wide and deep political foundations." In short, the current international system is "hard to overturn and easy to join." Top Chinese officials offer repeated assurances that China is intent on peacefully rising to great power status. A stable, nonthreatening international order is what they want because it allows China to focus on domestic development and modernization.

The essay explaining China's development approach is by Zheng Bijian, a high-level Chinese official and a chief proponent of China's peaceful rise. China's target is to achieve a "modernized, medium-level developed country" of 1.5 billion by 2050. To get there, Zheng Bijian says three big challenges must be met—a shortage of natural resources, a lack of coordination between economic and social development and heavy environmental pollution. CFR Fellow Elizabeth C. Economy warns that China's environmental problems are mounting. Air pollution levels are endangering the health of millions of Chinese and much of the country's land is rapidly turning into desert. Economy argues that Chinese officials have been unwilling to "pay the political and economic price" of managing environmental problems while fostering a thriving economy. John L. Thornton, a professor at Tsinghua University, surveys some of the democratizing changes in Chinese law, media, local elections, and the judiciary. For those who do not challenge the political system, life has improved. Still, severe constraints remain due to corruption, arbitrary governance, and limited freedom of expression and association.

In separate essays, economist C. Fred Bergsten and former treasury secretary Henry M. Paulson, Jr., make the case for a strategic economic relationship for the benefit of the global economy as well as for China and the United States. Elizabeth Economy and CFR Fellow Adam Segal add their voices of caution on embracing a formal G-2 top economic relationship. As the authors point out, there remain many hurdles to a consistently constructive relationship with China. "If the United States wants to move its relationship with China forward for the next 30 years, it needs the rest of the world, not just China, on board." The two remaining essays by scholars Stephen Kotkin and Bruce Gilley respectively assess the status of Chinese-Russian relations and Chinese-Taiwanese relations. China has managed to preserve a working relationship with Russia even after switching its strategic relationship to the United States. As for Taiwan, it is broadening the integration of its domestic interests with China's in the hope of sustaining Pacific relations.

In an effort to reach out to a broader audience, *Foreign Affairs* is pleased to present this collection, in both print and digital format.

China's "Peaceful Rise" to Great-Power Status

Zheng Bijian

SEPTEMBER/OCTOBER 2005

GETTING THE FACTS RIGHT

China's rapid development has attracted worldwide attention in recent years. The implications of various aspects of China's rise, from its expanding influence and military muscle to its growing demand for energy supplies, are being heatedly debated in the international community as well as within China. Correctly understanding China's achievements and its path toward greater development is thus crucial.

Since starting to open up and reform its economy in 1978, China has averaged 9.4 percent annual GDP growth, one of the highest growth rates in the world. In 1978, it accounted for less than one percent of the world economy, and its total foreign trade was worth $20.6 billion. Today, it accounts for four percent of the world economy and has foreign trade worth $851 billion—the third-largest national total in the world. China has

ZHENG BIJIAN is Chair of the China Reform Forum, a nongovernmental and nonprofit academic organization that provides research on and analysis of domestic, international, and development issues related to China. He has drafted key reports for five Chinese national party congresses and held senior posts in academic and party organizations in China.

also attracted hundreds of billions of dollars of foreign investment and more than a trillion dollars of domestic nonpublic
investment. A dozen years ago, China barely had mobile tele-
communications services. Now it claims more than 300 million mobile-phone subscribers, more than any other nation. As
of June 2004, nearly 100 million people there had access to the
Internet.

Indeed, China has achieved the goal it set for itself in 1978: it
has significantly improved the well-being of its people, although
its development has often been narrow and uneven. The last 27
years of reform and growth have also shown the world the mag-
nitude of China's labor force, creativity, and purchasing power;
its commitment to development; and its degree of national
cohesion. Once all of its potential is mobilized, its contribution
to the world as an engine of growth will be unprecedented.

One should not, however, lose sight of the other side of the
coin. Economic growth alone does not provide a full picture of
a country's development. China has a population of 1.3 billion.
Any small difficulty in its economic or social development, spread
over this vast group, could become a huge problem. And China's
population has not yet peaked; it is not projected to decline until
it reaches 1.5 billion in 2030. Moreover, China's economy is still
just one-seventh the size of the United States' and one-third the
size of Japan's. In per capita terms, China remains a low-income
developing country, ranked roughly 100th in the world. Its
impact on the world economy is still limited.

The formidable development challenges still facing China
stem from the constraints it faces in pulling its population out
of poverty. The scarcity of natural resources available to support such a huge population—especially energy, raw materials, and water—is increasingly an obstacle, especially when
the efficiency of use and the rate of recycling of those materials are low. China's per capita water resources are one-fourth
of the amount of the world average, and its per capita area of

cultivatable farmland is 40 percent of the world average. China's oil, natural gas, copper, and aluminum resources in per capita terms amount to 8.3 percent, 4.1 percent, 25.5 percent, and 9.7 percent of the respective world averages.

SETTING THE PRIORITIES

For the next few decades, the Chinese nation will be preoccupied with securing a more comfortable and decent life for its people. Since the Third Plenary Session of the Eleventh Central Committee of the Chinese Communist Party, held in 1978, the Chinese leadership has concentrated on economic development. Through its achievements so far, China has blazed a new strategic path that suits its national conditions while conforming to the tides of history. This path toward modernization can be called "the development path to a peaceful rise." Some emerging powers in modern history have plundered other countries' resources through invasion, colonization, expansion, or even large-scale wars of aggression. China's emergence thus far has been driven by capital, technology, and resources acquired through peaceful means.

The most significant strategic choice the Chinese have made was to embrace economic globalization rather than detach themselves from it. In the late 1970s, when the new technological revolution and a new wave of economic globalization were unfolding with great momentum, Beijing grasped the trend and reversed the erroneous practices of the Cultural Revolution. On the basis of the judgment that China's development would depend on its place in an open world, Deng Xiaoping and other Chinese leaders decided to seize the historic opportunity and shift the focus of their work to economic development. They carried out reforms meant to open up and foster domestic markets and tap into international ones. They implemented the household contracting system in rural areas and opened up 14 coastal cities, thus ushering in a period of economic takeoff.

In the 1990s, China once again confronted a strategic choice, due to the Asian financial crisis and the subsequent struggle between the forces for and against globalization. China's decision to participate in economic globalization was facing a serious challenge. But by carefully weighing the advantages and disadvantages of economic openness and drawing lessons from recent history, Beijing decided to open up China even more, by joining the World Trade Organization and deepening economic reform at home.

China has based its modernization process mainly on its domestic resources. It has relied on ideological and institutional innovations and on industrial restructuring. By exploring the growing domestic market and transferring the huge personal savings of its citizens into investment, China has infused its economy with new momentum. Its citizens' capacities are being upgraded and its technological progress expedited. Even while attempting to learn from and absorb useful products from other societies, including those of the advanced capitalist countries, China has maintained its independence and self-reliance.

In pursuing the goal of rising in peace, the Chinese leadership has strived for improving China's relations with all the nations of the world. Despite the ups and downs in U.S.-Chinese relations over the years, as well as other dramatic changes in international politics, such as the collapse of the Soviet Union, Beijing has stuck to the belief that there are more opportunities than challenges for China in today's international environment.

THE ROAD AHEAD

According to China's strategic plans, it will take another 45 years—until 2050—before it can be called a modernized, medium-level developed country. China will face three big challenges before it gets there. As described above, China's shortage of resources poses the first problem. The second is environmental: pollution, waste, and a low rate of recycling together present a major obstacle to sustainable development. The third is a lack of coordination between economic and social development.

This last challenge is reflected in a series of tensions Beijing must confront: between high GDP growth and social progress, between upgrading technology and increasing job opportunities, between keeping development momentum in the coastal areas and speeding up development in the interior, between fostering urbanization and nurturing agricultural areas, between narrowing the gap between the rich and the poor and maintaining economic vitality and efficiency, between attracting more foreign investment and enhancing the competitiveness of indigenous enterprises, between deepening reform and preserving social stability, between opening domestic markets and solidifying independence, between promoting market-oriented competition and taking care of disadvantaged people. To cope with these dilemmas successfully, a number of well-coordinated policies are needed to foster development that is both faster and more balanced.

The policies the Chinese government has been carrying out, and will continue to carry out, in the face of these three great challenges can be summarized as three grand strategies—or "three transcendences."

The first strategy is to transcend the old model of industrialization and to advance a new one. The old industrialization was characterized by rivalry for resources in bloody wars and by high investment, high consumption of energy, and high pollution. Were China to follow this path, it would harm both others and itself. China is instead determined to forge a new path of industrialization based on technology, economic efficiency, low consumption of natural resources relative to the size of its population, low environmental pollution, and the optimal allocation of human resources. The Chinese government is trying to find new ways to reduce the percentage of the country's imported energy sources and to rely more on China's own. The objective is to build a "society of thrift."

The second strategy is to transcend the traditional ways for great powers to emerge, as well as the Cold War mentality that defined international relations along ideological lines. China will not follow the path of Germany leading up to World War I or those of Germany and Japan leading up to World War II, when these countries violently plundered resources and pursued hegemony. Neither will China follow the path of the great powers vying for global domination during the Cold War. Instead, China will transcend ideological differences to strive for peace, development, and cooperation with all countries of the world.

The third strategy is to transcend outdated modes of social control and to construct a harmonious socialist society. The functions of the Chinese government have been gradually transformed, with self-governance supplementing state administration. China is strengthening its democratic institutions and the rule of law and trying to build a stable society based on a spiritual civilization. A great number of ideological and moral-education programs have been launched.

Several dynamic forces are noticeable in the carrying out of the three strategies. For example, there are numerous clusters of vigorously developing cities in the coastal areas of eastern and southern China, and similar clusters are emerging in the central and western regions. They constitute the main engines of growth, are the major manufacturing and trading centers, and absorb surplus rural labor. They also have high productivity, advanced culture, and accumulated international experience that the rest of China can emulate and learn from. The expansion of China's middle-income strata and the growing need for international markets come mainly from these regions.

Zheng Bijian

China's surplus of rural workers, who have strong aspirations to escape poverty, is another force that is pushing Chinese society into industrial civilization. About ten million rural Chinese migrate to urban areas each year in an orderly and protected way. They both provide Chinese cities with new productivity and new markets and help end the backwardness of rural areas. Innovations in science and technology and culture are also driving China toward modernization and prosperity in the twenty-first century.

The Chinese government has set up targets for development for the next 50 years. This period is divided into three stages. In the first stage—2000 to 2010—total GDP is to be doubled. In the second stage, ending in 2020, total GDP is to be doubled again, at which point China's per capita GDP is expected to reach $3,000. In the third, from 2020 to 2050, China will continue to advance until it becomes a prosperous, democratic, and civilized socialist country. By that time, China will have shaken off underdevelopment and will be on a par with the middle rung of advanced nations. It can then claim to have succeeded in achieving a "peaceful rise."

IMPACT ON THE WORLD

China's peaceful rise will further open its economy so that its population can serve as a growing market for the rest of the world, thus providing increased opportunities for—rather than posing a threat to—the international community. A few figures illustrate China's current contribution to global trade: in 2004, China's imports from members of the Association of Southeast Asian Nations increased by 33.1 percent, from Japan by 27.3 percent, from India by 80 percent, from the European Union by 28 percent, and from the United States by 31.9 percent.

China is not the only power that seeks a peaceful rise. China's economic integration into East Asia has contributed to the shaping of an East Asian community that may rise in peace as a whole. And it would not be in China's interest to exclude the United States from the process. In fact, Beijing wants Washington to play a positive role in the region's security as well as economic affairs. The beginning of the twenty-first century is seeing a number of countries rising through different means, while following different models, and at different paces. At the same time, the developed countries are further developing themselves. This is a trend to be welcomed.

China does not seek hegemony or predominance in world affairs. It advocates a new international political and economic order, one that can be achieved through incremental reforms and the democratization of international relations. China's development depends on world peace—a peace that its development will in turn reinforce.

The Great Leap Backward?

Elizabeth C. Economy

China's environmental problems are mounting. Water pollution and water scarcity are burdening the economy, rising levels of air pollution are endangering the health of millions of Chinese, and much of the country's land is rapidly turning into desert. China has become a world leader in air and water pollution and land degradation and a top contributor to some of the world's most vexing global environmental problems, such as the illegal timber trade, marine pollution, and climate change. As China's pollution woes increase, so, too, do the risks to its economy, public health, social stability, and international reputation. As Pan Yue, a vice minister of China's State Environmental Protection Administration (SEPA), warned in 2005, "The [economic] miracle will end soon because the environment can no longer keep pace."

With the 2008 Olympics around the corner, China's leaders have ratcheted up their rhetoric, setting ambitious environmental targets, announcing greater levels of environmental investment, and exhorting business leaders and local officials to clean up their backyards. The rest of the world seems to accept that

ELIZABETH C. ECONOMY is C. V. Starr Senior Fellow and Director for Asia Studies at the Council on Foreign Relations and the author of *The River Runs Black: The Environmental Challenges to China's Future*.

Beijing has charted a new course: as China declares itself open for environmentally friendly business, officials in the United States, the European Union, and Japan are asking not whether to invest but how much.

Unfortunately, much of this enthusiasm stems from the widespread but misguided belief that what Beijing says goes. The central government sets the country's agenda, but it does not control all aspects of its implementation. In fact, local officials rarely heed Beijing's environmental mandates, preferring to concentrate their energies and resources on further advancing economic growth. The truth is that turning the environmental situation in China around will require something far more difficult than setting targets and spending money; it will require revolutionary bottom-up political and economic reforms.

For one thing, China's leaders need to make it easy for local officials and factory owners to do the right thing when it comes to the environment by giving them the right incentives. At the same time, they must loosen the political restrictions they have placed on the courts, nongovernmental organizations (NGOs), and the media in order to enable these groups to become independent enforcers of environmental protection. The international community, for its part, must focus more on assisting reform and less on transferring cutting-edge technologies and developing demonstration projects. Doing so will mean diving into the trenches to work with local Chinese officials, factory owners, and environmental NGOs; enlisting international NGOs to help with education and enforcement policies; and persuading multinational corporations (MNCs) to use their economic leverage to ensure that their Chinese partners adopt the best environmental practices.

Without such a clear-eyed understanding not only of what China wants but also of what it needs, China will continue to have one of the world's worst environmental records, and the Chinese people and the rest of the world will pay the price.

SINS OF EMISSION

China's rapid development, often touted as an economic miracle, has become an environmental disaster. Record growth necessarily requires the gargantuan consumption of resources, but in China energy use has been especially unclean and inefficient, with dire consequences for the country's air, land, and water.

The coal that has powered China's economic growth, for example, is also choking its people. Coal provides about 70 percent of China's energy needs: the country consumed some 2.4 billion tons in 2006—more than the United States, Japan, and the United Kingdom combined. In 2000, China anticipated doubling its coal consumption by 2020; it is now expected to have done so by the end of this year. Consumption in China is huge partly because it is inefficient: as one Chinese official told *Der Spiegel* in early 2006, "To produce goods worth $10,000 we need seven times the resources used by Japan, almost six times the resources used by the U.S. and—a particular source of embarrassment—almost three times the resources used by India."

Meanwhile, this reliance on coal is devastating China's environment. The country is home to 16 of the world's 20 most polluted cities, and four of the worst off among them are in the coal-rich province of Shanxi, in northeastern China. As much as 90 percent of China's sulfur dioxide emissions and 50 percent of its particulate emissions are the result of coal use. Particulates are responsible for respiratory problems among the population, and acid rain, which is caused by sulfur dioxide emissions, falls on one-quarter of China's territory and on one-third of its agricultural land, diminishing agricultural output and eroding buildings.

Yet coal use may soon be the least of China's air-quality problems. The transportation boom poses a growing challenge to China's air quality. Chinese developers are laying more than

52,700 miles of new highways throughout the country. Some 14,000 new cars hit China's roads each day. By 2020, China is expected to have 130 million cars, and by 2050—or perhaps as early as 2040—it is expected to have even more cars than the United States. Beijing already pays a high price for this boom. In a 2006 survey, Chinese respondents rated Beijing the 15th most livable city in China, down from the 4th in 2005, with the drop due largely to increased traffic and pollution. Levels of airborne particulates are now six times higher in Beijing than in New York City.

China's grand-scale urbanization plans will aggravate matters. China's leaders plan to relocate 400 million people—equivalent to well over the entire population of the United States—to newly developed urban centers between 2000 and 2030. In the process, they will erect half of all the buildings expected to be constructed in the world during that period. This is a troubling prospect considering that Chinese buildings are not energy efficient—in fact, they are roughly two and a half times less so than those in Germany. Furthermore, newly urbanized Chinese, who use air conditioners, televisions, and refrigerators, consume about three and a half times more energy than do their rural counterparts. And although China is one of the world's largest producer of solar cells, compact fluorescent lights, and energy-efficient windows, these are produced mostly for export. Unless more of these energy-saving goods stay at home, the building boom will result in skyrocketing energy consumption and pollution.

China's land has also suffered from unfettered development and environmental neglect. Centuries of deforestation, along with the overgrazing of grasslands and overcultivation of cropland, have left much of China's north and northwest seriously degraded. In the past half century, moreover, forests and farmland have had to make way for industry and sprawling cities, resulting in diminishing crop yields, a loss in biodiversity, and local climatic change. The Gobi Desert, which now engulfs much of western and northern China, is spreading by about 1,900 square miles annually; some reports say that despite Beijing's aggressive reforestation efforts, one-quarter of the entire country is now desert. China's State Forestry Administration estimates that desertification has hurt some 400 million Chinese, turning tens of millions of them into environmental refugees, in search of new homes and jobs. Meanwhile, much of China's arable soil is contaminated, raising concerns about food safety. As much as ten percent of China's farmland is believed to be polluted, and every year 12 million tons of grain are contaminated with heavy metals absorbed from the soil.

WATER HAZARD

And then there is the problem of access to clean water. Although China holds the fourth-largest freshwater resources in the world (after Brazil, Russia, and Canada), skyrocketing demand, overuse, inefficiencies, pollution, and unequal distribution have produced a situation in which two-thirds of China's approximately 660 cities have less water than they need and 110 of them suffer severe shortages. According to Ma Jun, a leading Chinese water expert, several cities near Beijing and Tianjin, in the northeastern region of the country, could run out of water in five to seven years.

Growing demand is part of the problem, of course, but so is enormous waste. The agricultural sector lays claim to 66 percent of the water China consumes, mostly for irrigation, and manages to waste more than half of that. Chinese industries are highly inefficient: they generally use 10–20 percent more water than do their counterparts in developed countries. Urban China is an especially huge squanderer: it loses up to 20 percent of the water it consumes through leaky pipes—a problem that China's Ministry of Construction has pledged to address in the next two to three years. As urbanization proceeds and incomes rise, the Chinese, much like people in Europe and the United States, have become larger consumers of water: they take lengthy showers, use washing machines and dishwashers, and purchase second homes with lawns that need to be watered. Water consumption in Chinese cities jumped by 6.6 percent during 2004–5. China's plundering of its ground-water reserves, which has created massive underground tunnels, is causing a corollary problem: some of China's wealthiest cities are sinking—in the case of Shanghai and Tianjin, by more than six feet during the past decade and a half. In Beijing, subsidence has destroyed factories, buildings, and underground pipelines and is threatening the city's main international airport.

Pollution is also endangering China's water supplies. China's ground water, which provides 70 percent of the country's total drinking water, is under threat from a variety of sources, such as polluted surface water, hazardous waste sites, and pesticides and fertilizers. According to one report by the government-run Xinhua News Agency, the aquifers in 90 percent of Chinese cities are polluted. More than 75 percent of the river water flowing through China's urban areas is considered unsuitable for drinking or fishing, and the Chinese government deems about 30 percent of the river water throughout the country to be unfit for use in agriculture or industry. As a result, nearly 700 million people drink water contaminated with animal and human waste. The World Bank has found that the failure to provide fully two-thirds of the rural population with piped water is a leading cause of death among children under the age of five and is responsible for as much as 11 percent of the cases of gastrointestinal cancer in China.

One of the problems is that although China has plenty of laws and regulations designed to ensure clean water, factory owners and local officials do not enforce them. A 2005 survey of 509 cities revealed that only 23 percent of factories properly treated sewage before disposing of it. According to another report, today one-third of all industrial wastewater in China and two-thirds of household sewage are released untreated. Recent Chinese studies of two of the country's most important sources of water—the Yangtze and Yellow rivers—illustrate the growing challenge. The Yangtze River, which stretches all the way from the Tibetan Plateau to Shanghai, receives 40 percent of the country's sewage, 80 percent of it untreated. In 2007, the Chinese government announced that it was delaying, in part because of pollution, the development of a $60 billion plan to divert the river in order to supply the water-starved cities of Beijing and Tianjin. The Yellow River supplies water to more than 150 million people and 15 percent of China's agricultural land, but two-thirds of its water is considered unsafe to drink and 10 percent of its water is classified as sewage. In early 2007, Chinese officials announced that over one-third of the fish species native to the Yellow River had become extinct due to damming or pollution.

China's leaders are also increasingly concerned about how climate change may exacerbate their domestic environmental situation. In the spring of 2007, Beijing released its first national assessment report on climate change, predicting a 30 percent drop in precipitation in three of China's seven major river regions—around the Huai, Liao, and Hai rivers—and a 37 percent decline in the country's wheat, rice, and corn yields in the second half of the century. It also predicted that the Yangtze and Yellow rivers, which derive much of their water from glaciers in Tibet, would overflow as the glaciers melted and then dry up. And both Chinese and international scientists now warn that due to rising sea levels, Shanghai could be submerged by 2050.

The Great Leap Backward?

COLLATERAL DAMAGE

China's environmental problems are already affecting the rest of the world. Japan and South Korea have long suffered from the acid rain produced by China's coal-fired power plants and from the eastbound dust storms that sweep across the Gobi Desert in the spring and dump toxic yellow dust on their land. Researchers in the United States are tracking dust, sulfur, soot, and trace metals as these travel across the Pacific from China. The U.S. Environmental Protection Agency estimates that on some days, 25 percent of the particulates in the atmosphere in Los Angeles originated in China.[1] Scientists have also traced rising levels of mercury deposits on U.S. soil back to coal-fired power plants and cement factories in China. (When ingested in significant quantities, mercury can cause birth defects and developmental problems.) Reportedly, 25–40 percent of all mercury emissions in the world come from China.

What China dumps into its waters is also polluting the rest of the world. According to the international NGO the World Wildlife Fund, China is now the largest polluter of the Pacific Ocean. As Liu Quangfeng, an adviser to the National People's Congress, put it, "Almost no river that flows into the Bo Hai [a sea along China's northern coast] is clean." China releases about 2.8 billion tons of contaminated water into the Bo Hai annually, and the content of heavy metal in the mud at the bottom of it is now 2,000 times as high as China's own official safety standard. The prawn catch has dropped by 90 percent over the past 15 years. In 2006, in the heavily industrialized southeastern provinces of Guangdong and Fujian, almost 8.3 billion tons

---

[1]The original Associated Press story that was the source for the statement was mistaken and has been corrected. In fact, the EPA, citing a model saying that Asia contributes about 30 percent of the background sulfate particulate matter in the western United States, estimates that Asia contributes about one percent of all particulate matter in Los Angeles.

of sewage were discharged into the ocean without treatment, a 60 percent increase from 2001. More than 80 percent of the East China Sea, one of the world's largest fisheries, is now rated unsuitable for fishing, up from 53 percent in 2000.

Furthermore, China is already attracting international attention for its rapidly growing contribution to climate change. According to a 2007 report from the Netherlands Environmental Assessment Agency, it has already surpassed the United States as the world's largest contributor of carbon dioxide, a leading greenhouse gas, to the atmosphere. Unless China rethinks its use of various sources of energy and adopts cutting-edge environmentally friendly technologies, warned Fatih Birol, the chief economist of the International Energy Agency, last April, in 25 years China will emit twice as much carbon dioxide as all the countries of the Organization for Economic Cooperation and Development combined.

China's close economic partners in the developing world face additional environmental burdens from China's economic activities. Chinese multinationals, which are exploiting natural resources in Africa, Latin America, and Southeast Asia in order to fuel China's continued economic rise, are devastating these regions' habitats in the process. China's hunger for timber has exploded over the past decade and a half, and particularly since 1998, when devastating floods led Beijing to crack down on domestic logging. China's timber imports more than tripled between 1993 and 2005. According to the World Wildlife Fund, China's demand for timber, paper, and pulp will likely increase by 33 percent between 2005 and 2010.

China is already the largest importer of illegally logged timber in the world: an estimated 50 percent of its timber imports are reportedly illegal. Illegal logging is especially damaging to the environment because it often targets rare old-growth forests, endangers biodiversity, and ignores sustainable forestry practices. In 2006, the government of Cambodia, for example, ignored its own laws and awarded China's Wuzhishan LS Group a 99-year concession that was 20 times as large as the size permitted by Cambodian law. The company's practices, including the spraying of large amounts of herbicides, have prompted repeated protests by local Cambodians. According to the international NGO Global Witness, Chinese companies have destroyed large parts of the forests along the Chinese-Myanmar border and are now moving deeper into Myanmar's forests in their search for timber. In many instances, illicit logging activity takes place with the active support of corrupt local officials. Central government officials in Myanmar and Indonesia, countries where China's loggers are active, have protested such arrangements to Beijing, but relief has been limited. These activities, along with those of Chinese mining and energy companies, raise serious environmental concerns for many local populations in the developing world.

SPOILING THE PARTY

In the view of China's leaders, however, damage to the environment itself is a secondary problem. Of greater concern to them are its indirect effects: the threat it poses to the continuation of the Chinese economic miracle and to public health, social stability, and the country's international reputation. Taken together, these challenges could undermine the authority of the Communist Party.

China's leaders are worried about the environment's impact on the economy. Several studies conducted both inside and outside China estimate that environmental degradation and pollution cost the Chinese economy between 8 percent and 12 percent of GDP annually. The Chinese media frequently publish the results of studies on the impact of pollution on agriculture, industrial output, or public health: water pollution costs of $35.8 billion one year, air pollution costs of $27.5 billion another, and on and on with weather disasters ($26.5 billion), acid rain ($13.3 billion), desertification ($6 billion), or crop damage from soil pollution ($2.5 billion). The city of Chongqing, which sits on the banks of the Yangtze River, estimates that dealing with the effects of water pollution on its agriculture and public health costs as much as 4.3 percent of the city's annual gross product. Shanxi Province has watched its coal resources fuel the rest of the country while it pays the price in withered trees, contaminated air and water, and land subsidence. Local authorities there estimate the costs of environmental degradation and pollution at 10.9 percent of the province's annual gross product and have called on Beijing to compensate the province for its "contribution and sacrifice."

China's Ministry of Public Health is also sounding the alarm with increasing urgency. In a survey of 30 cities and 78 counties released in the spring, the ministry blamed worsening air and water pollution for dramatic increases in the incidence of cancer throughout the country: a 19 percent rise in urban areas and a 23 percent rise in rural areas since 2005. One research institute affiliated with SEPA has put the total number of premature deaths in China caused by respiratory diseases related to air pollution at 400,000 a year. But this may be a conservative estimate: according to a joint research project by the World Bank and the Chinese government released this year, the total number of such deaths is 750,000 a year. (Beijing is said not to have wanted to release the latter figure for fear of inciting social unrest.) Less well documented but potentially even more devastating is the health impact of China's polluted water. Today, fully 190 million Chinese are sick from drinking contaminated water. All along China's major rivers, villages report skyrocketing rates of diarrheal diseases, cancer, tumors, leukemia, and stunted growth.

Social unrest over these issues is rising. In the spring of 2006, China's top environmental official, Zhou Shengxian, announced that there had been 51,000 pollution-related protests in 2005, which amounts to almost 1,000 protests each week. Citizen complaints about the environment, expressed on official hotlines and in letters to local officials, are increasing at a rate of 30 percent a year; they will likely top 450,000 in 2007. But few of them are resolved satisfactorily, and so people throughout the country are increasingly taking to the streets. For several months in 2006, for example, the residents of six neighboring villages in Gansu Province held repeated protests against zinc and iron smelters that they believed were poisoning them. Fully half of the 4,000–5,000 villagers exhibited lead-related illnesses, ranging from vitamin D deficiency to neurological problems.

Many pollution-related marches are relatively small and peaceful. But when such demonstrations fail, the protesters sometimes resort to violence. After trying for two years to get redress by petitioning local, provincial, and even central government officials for spoiled crops and poisoned air, in the spring of 2005, 30,000–40,000 villagers from Zhejiang Province swarmed 13 chemical plants, broke windows and overturned buses, attacked government officials, and torched police cars. The government sent in 10,000 members of the People's Armed Police in response. The plants were ordered to close down, and several environmental activists who attempted to monitor the plants' compliance with these orders were later arrested. China's leaders have generally managed to prevent— if sometimes violently—discontent over environmental issues from spreading across provincial boundaries or morphing into calls for broader political reform.

In the face of such problems, China's leaders have recently injected a new urgency into their rhetoric concerning the need to protect the country's environment. On paper, this has translated into an aggressive strategy to increase investment in environmental protection, set ambitious targets for the reduction of pollution and energy intensity (the amount of energy used to produce a unit of GDP), and introduce new environmentally friendly technologies. In 2005, Beijing set out a number of impressive targets for its next five-year plan: by 2010, it wants 10 percent of the nation's power to come from renewable energy sources, energy intensity to have been reduced by 20 percent and key pollutants such as sulfur dioxide by 10 percent, water consumption to have decreased by 30 percent, and investment in environmental protection to have increased from 1.3 percent to 1.6 percent of GDP. Premier Wen Jiabao has issued a stern warning to local officials to shut down some of the plants in the most energy-intensive industries—power generation and aluminum, copper, steel, coke and coal, and cement production—and to slow the growth of other industries by denying them tax breaks and other production incentives.

These goals are laudable—even breathtaking in some respects—but history suggests that only limited optimism is warranted; achieving such targets has proved elusive in the past. In 2001, the Chinese government pledged to cut sulfur dioxide emissions by 10 percent between 2002 and 2005. Instead, emissions rose by 27 percent. Beijing is already encountering difficulties reaching its latest goals: for instance, it has failed to meet its first target for reducing energy intensity and pollution. Despite warnings from Premier Wen, the six industries that were slated to slow down posted a 20.6 percent increase in output during the first quarter of 2007—a 6.6 percent jump from the same period last year. According to one senior executive with the Indian wind-power firm Suzlon Energy, only 37 percent of the wind-power projects the Chinese government approved in 2004 have been built. Perhaps worried that yet another target would fall by the wayside, in early 2007, Beijing revised its announced goal of reducing the country's water consumption by 30 percent by 2010 to just 20 percent.

Even the Olympics are proving to be a challenge. Since Beijing promised in 2001 to hold a "green Olympics" in 2008, the

International Olympic Committee has pulled out all the stops. Beijing is now ringed with rows of newly planted trees, hybrid taxis and buses are roaming its streets (some of which are soon to be lined with solar-powered lamps), the most heavily polluting factories have been pushed outside the city limits, and the Olympic dormitories are models of energy efficiency. Yet in key respects, Beijing has failed to deliver. City officials are backtracking from their pledge to provide safe tap water to all of Beijing for the Olympics; they now say that they will provide it only for residents of the Olympic Village. They have announced drastic stopgap measures for the duration of the games, such as banning one million of the city's three million cars from the city's streets and halting production at factories in and around Beijing (some of them are resisting). Whatever progress city authorities have managed over the past six years— such as increasing the number of days per year that the city's air is deemed to be clean—is not enough to ensure that the air will be clean for the Olympic Games. Preparing for the Olympics has come to symbolize the intractability of China's environmental challenges and the limits of Beijing's approach to addressing them.

PROBLEMS WITH THE LOCALS

Clearly, something has got to give. The costs of inaction to China's economy, public health, and international reputation are growing. And perhaps more important, social discontent is rising. The Chinese people have clearly run out of patience with the government's inability or unwillingness to turn the environmental situation around. And the government is well aware of the increasing potential for environmental protest to ignite broader social unrest.

One event this spring particularly alarmed China's leaders. For several days in May in the coastal city of Xiamen, after months of mounting opposition to the planned construction of a $1.4 billion petrochemical plant nearby, students and professors at Xiamen University, among others, are said to have sent out a million mobile-phone text messages calling on their fellow citizens to take to the streets on June 1. That day, and the following, protesters reportedly numbering between 7,000 and 20,000 marched peacefully through the city, some defying threats of expulsion from school or from the Communist Party. The protest was captured on video and uploaded to YouTube. One video featured a haunting voice-over that linked the Xiamen demonstration to an ongoing environmental crisis near Tai Hu, a lake some 400 miles away (a large bloom of blue-green algae caused by industrial wastewater and sewage dumped in the lake had contaminated the water supply of the city of Wuxi). It also referred to the Tiananmen Square protest of 1989. The Xiamen march, the narrator said, was perhaps "the first genuine parade since Tiananmen."

In response, city authorities did stay the construction of the plant, but they also launched an all-out campaign to discredit the protesters and their videos. Still, more comments about the protest and calls not to forget Tiananmen appeared on various Web sites. Such messages, posted openly and accessible to all Chinese, represent the Chinese leadership's greatest fear, namely, that its failure to protect the environment may someday serve as the catalyst for broad-based demands for political change.

Such public demonstrations are also evidence that China's environmental challenges cannot be met with only impressive targets and more investment. They must be tackled with a fundamental reform of how the country does business and protects the environment. So far, Beijing has structured its environmental protection efforts in much the same way that it has pursued economic growth: by granting local authorities and factory owners wide decision-making power and by actively courting the international community and Chinese NGOs for their expertise while carefully monitoring their activities.

Consider, for example, China's most important environmental authority, SEPA, in Beijing. SEPA has become a wellspring of China's most innovative environmental policies: it has promoted an environmental impact assessment law; a law requiring local officials to release information about environmental disasters, pollution statistics, and the names of known polluters to the public; an experiment to calculate the costs of environmental degradation and pollution to the country's GDP; and an all-out effort to halt over 100 large-scale infrastructure projects that had proceeded without proper environmental impact assessments. But SEPA operates with barely 300 full-time professional staff in the capital and only a few hundred employees spread throughout the country. (The U.S. Environmental Protection Agency has a staff of almost 9,000 in Washington, D.C., alone.) And authority for enforcing SEPA's mandates rests overwhelmingly with local officials and the local environmental protection officials they oversee. In some cases, this has allowed for exciting experimentation. In the eastern province of Jiangsu, for instance, the World Bank and the Natural Resources Defense Council have launched the Greenwatch program, which grades 12,000 factories according to their compliance with standards for industrial wastewater treatment and discloses both the ratings and the reasons for them. More often, however, China's highly decentralized system has meant limited progress: only seven to ten percent of China's more than 660 cities meet the standards required to receive the designation of National Model Environmental City from SEPA. According to Wang Canfa, one of China's top environmental lawyers, barely ten percent of China's environmental laws and regulations are actually enforced.

One of the problems is that local officials have few incentives to place a priority on environmental protection. Even as Beijing touts the need to protect the environment, Premier Wen has called for quadrupling the Chinese economy by 2020. The price of water is rising in some cities, such as Beijing, but in many others it remains as low as 20 percent of the replacement cost. That ensures that factories and municipalities have little reason to invest in wastewater treatment or other water-conservation efforts. Fines for polluting are so low that factory managers often prefer to pay them rather than adopt costlier pollution-control technologies. One manager of a coal-fired power plant explained to a Chinese reporter in 2005 that he was ignoring a recent edict mandating that all new power plants use desulfurization equipment because the technology cost as much as would 15 years' worth of fines.

Local governments also turn a blind eye to serious pollution problems out of self-interest. Officials sometimes have a direct financial stake in factories or personal relationships with their owners. And the local environmental protection bureaus tasked with guarding against such corruption must report to the local governments, making them easy targets for political pressure. In recent years, the Chinese media have uncovered cases in which local officials have put pressure on the courts, the press, or even hospitals to prevent the wrongdoings of factories from coming to light. (Just this year, in the province of Zhejiang, officials reportedly promised factories with an output of $1.2 million or more that they would not be subjected to government inspections without the factories' prior approval.)

Moreover, local officials frequently divert environmental protection funds and spend them on unrelated or ancillary endeavors. The Chinese Academy for Environmental Planning, which reports to SEPA, disclosed this year that only half of the 1.3 percent of the country's annual GDP dedicated to environmental protection between 2001 and 2005 had found its way to legitimate projects. According to the study, about 60 percent of the environmental protection funds spent in urban areas during that period went into the creation of, among other things, parks, factory production lines, gas stations, and sewage-treatment plants rather than into waste- or wastewater-treatment facilities.

Many local officials also thwart efforts to hold them accountable for their failure to protect the environment. In 2005, SEPA launched the "Green GDP" campaign, a project designed to calculate the costs of environmental degradation and pollution to local economies and provide a basis for evaluating the performance of local officials both according to their economic stewardship and according to how well they protect the environment. Several provinces balked, however, worried that the numbers would reveal the extent of the damage suffered by the environment. SEPA's partner in the campaign, the National Bureau of Statistics of China, also undermined the effort by announcing that it did not possess the tools to do Green GDP accounting accurately and that in any case it did not believe officials should be evaluated on such a basis. After releasing a partial report in September 2006, the NBS has refused to release this year's findings to the public.

Another problem is that many Chinese companies see little direct value in ratcheting up their environmental protection efforts. The computer manufacturer Lenovo and the appliance manufacturer Haier have received high marks for taking creative environmental measures, and the solar energy company Suntech has become a leading exporter of solar cells. But a recent poll found that only 18 percent of Chinese companies believed that they could thrive economically while doing the right thing environmentally. Another poll of business executives found that an overwhelming proportion of them do not understand the benefits of responsible corporate behavior, such as environmental protection, or consider the requirements too burdensome.

Elizabeth C. Economy

NOT GOOD ENOUGH

The limitations of the formal authorities tasked with environmental protection in China have led the country's leaders to seek assistance from others outside the bureaucracy. Over the past 15 years or so, China's NGOs, the Chinese media, and the international community have become central actors in the country's bid to rescue its environment. But the Chinese government remains wary of them.

China's homegrown environmental activists and their allies in the media have become the most potent—and potentially explosive—force for environmental change in China. From four or five NGOs devoted primarily to environmental education and biodiversity protection in the mid-1990s, the Chinese environmental movement has grown to include thousands of NGOs, run primarily by dynamic Chinese in their 30s and 40s. These groups now routinely expose polluting factories to the central government, sue for the rights of villagers poisoned by contaminated water or air, give seed money to small newer NGOs throughout the country, and go undercover to expose multinationals that ignore international environmental standards. They often protest via letters to the government, campaigns on the Internet, and editorials in Chinese newspapers. The media are an important ally in this fight: they shame polluters, uncover environmental abuse, and highlight environmental protection successes.

Beijing has come to tolerate NGOs and media outlets that play environmental watchdog at the local level, but it remains vigilant in making sure that certain limits are not crossed, and especially that the central government is not directly criticized. The penalties for misjudging these boundaries can be severe. Wu Lihong worked for 16 years to address the pollution in Tai Hu (which recently spawned blue-green algae), gathering evidence that has forced almost 200 factories to close. Although in

2005 Beijing honored Wu as one of the country's top environmentalists, he was beaten by local thugs several times during the course of his investigations, and in 2006 the government of the town of Yixing arrested him on dubious charges of blackmail. And Yu Xiaogang, the 2006 winner of the prestigious Goldman Environmental Prize, honoring grass-roots environmentalists, was forbidden to travel abroad in retaliation for educating villagers about the potential downsides of a proposed dam relocation in Yunnan Province.

The Chinese government's openness to environmental cooperation with the international community is also fraught. Beijing has welcomed bilateral agreements for technology development or financial assistance for demonstration projects, but it is concerned about other endeavors. On the one hand, it lauds international environmental NGOs for their contributions to China's environmental protection efforts. On the other hand, it fears that some of them will become advocates for democratization.

The government also subjects MNCs to an uncertain operating environment. Many corporations have responded to the government's calls that they assume a leading role in the country's environmental protection efforts by deploying top-of-the-line environmental technologies, financing environmental education in Chinese schools, undertaking community-based efforts, and raising operating standards in their industries. Coca-Cola, for example, recently pledged to become a net-zero consumer of water, and Wal-Mart is set to launch a nationwide education and sales initiative to promote the use of energy-efficient compact fluorescent bulbs. Sometimes, MNCs have been rewarded with awards or significant publicity. But in the past two years, Chinese officials (as well as local NGOs) have adopted a much tougher stance toward them, arguing at times that MNCs have turned China into the pollution capital of the world. On issues such as electronic waste, the detractors have a point. But China's attacks, with Internet postings accusing MNCs of practicing "eco-colonialism," have become unjustifiably broad. Such antiforeign sentiment spiked in late 2006, after the release of a pollution map listing more than 3,000 factories that were violating water pollution standards. The 33 among them that supplied MNCs were immediately targeted in the media, while the other few thousand Chinese factories cited somehow escaped the frenzy. A few Chinese officials and activists privately acknowledge that domestic Chinese companies pollute far more than foreign companies, but it seems unlikely that the spotlight will move off MNCs in the near future. For now, it is simply more expedient to let international corporations bear the bulk of the blame.

FROM RED TO GREEN

Why is China unable to get its environmental house in order? Its top officials want what the United States, Europe, and Japan have: thriving economies with manageable environmental problems. But they are unwilling to pay the political and economic price to get there. Beijing's message to local officials continues to be that economic growth cannot be sacrificed to environmental protection—that the two objectives must go hand in hand.

This, however, only works sometimes. Greater energy efficiency can bring economic benefits, and investments to reduce pollution, such as in building wastewater-treatment plants, are expenses that can be balanced against the costs of losing crops to contaminated soil and having a sickly work force. Yet much of the time, charting a new environmental course comes with serious economic costs up front. Growth slows down in some industries or some regions. Some businesses are forced to close down. Developing pollution-treatment and pollution-prevention technologies requires serious investment. In fact, it is because they recognize these costs that local officials in China pursue their short-term economic interests first and for the most part ignore Beijing's directives to change their ways.

This is not an unusual problem. All countries suffer internal tugs of war over how to balance the short-term costs of improving environmental protection with the long-term costs of failing to do so. But China faces an additional burden. Its environmental problems stem as much from China's corrupt and undemocratic political system as from Beijing's continued focus on economic growth. Local officials and business leaders routinely—and with impunity—ignore environmental laws and regulations, abscond with environmental protection funds, and silence those who challenge them. Thus, improving the environment in China is not simply a matter of mandating pollution-control technologies; it is also a matter of reforming the country's political culture. Effective environmental protection requires transparent information, official accountability, and an independent legal system. But these features are the building blocks of a political system fundamentally different from that of China today, and so far there is little indication that China's leaders will risk the authority of the Communist Party on charting a new environmental course. Until the party is willing to open the door to such reform, it will not have the wherewithal to meet its ambitious environmental targets and lead a growing economy with manageable environmental problems.

Given this reality, the United States—and the rest of the world—will have to get much smarter about how to cooperate with China in order to assist its environmental protection efforts. Above all, the United States must devise a limited and coherent set of priorities. China's needs are vast, but its capacity is poor; therefore, launching one or two significant initiatives over the next five to ten years would do more good than a vast array of uncoordinated projects. These endeavors could focus on discrete issues, such as climate change or the illegal timber trade; institutional changes, such as strengthening the legal system in regard to China's environmental protection efforts; or broad reforms, such as promoting energy efficiency throughout the Chinese economy. Another key to an effective U.S.-Chinese partnership is U.S. leadership. Although U.S. NGOs and U.S.-based MNCs are often at the forefront of environmental policy and technological innovation, the U.S. government itself is not a world leader on key environmental concerns. Unless the United States improves its own policies and practices on, for example, climate change, the illegal timber trade, and energy efficiency, it will have little credibility or leverage to push China.

China, for its part, will undoubtedly continue to place a priority on gaining easy access to financial and technological assistance. Granting this, however, would be the wrong way to go. Joint efforts between the United States and China, such as the recently announced project to capture methane from 15 Chinese coal mines, are important, of course. But the systemic changes needed to set China on a new environmental trajectory necessitate a bottom-up overhaul. One way to start would be to promote energy efficiency in Chinese factories and buildings. Simply bringing these up to world standards would bring vast gains. International and Chinese NGOs, Chinese environmental protection bureaus, and MNCs could audit and rate Chinese factories based on how well their manufacturing processes and building standards met a set of energy-efficiency targets. Their scores (and the factors that determined them) could then be disclosed to the public via the Internet and the print media, and factories with subpar performances could be given the means to improve their practices.

A pilot program in Guangdong Province, which is run under the auspices of the U.S. consulate in Hong Kong, provides just such a mechanism. Factories that apply for energy audits can take out loans from participating banks to pay for efficiency upgrades, with the expectation that they will pay the loans back over time out of the savings they will realize from using fewer materials or conserving energy. Such programs should be encouraged and could be reinforced by requiring, for example, that the U.S.-based MNCs that worked with the participating factories rewarded those that met or exceeded the standards and penalized those that did not (the MNCs could either expand or reduce their orders, for example). NGOs and the media in China could also publicize the names of the factories that refused to cooperate. These initiatives would have the advantages of operating within the realities of China's environmental protection system, providing both incentives and disincentives to encourage factories to comply; strengthening the role of key actors such as NGOs, the media, and local environmental protection bureaus; and engaging new actors such as Chinese banks. It is likely that as with the Greenwatch program, factory owners and local officials not used to transparency would oppose such efforts, but if they were persuaded that full participation would bring more sales to MNCs and grow local economies, many of them would be more open to public disclosure.

Of course, much of the burden and the opportunity for China to revolutionize the way it reconciles environmental protection and economic development rests with the Chinese government itself. No amount of international assistance can transform China's domestic environment or its contribution to global environmental challenges. Real change will arise only from strong central leadership and the development of a system of incentives that make it easier for local officials and the Chinese people to embrace environmental protection. This will sometimes mean making tough economic choices.

Improvements to energy efficiency, of the type promoted by the program in Guangdong, are reforms of the low-hanging-fruit variety: they promise both economic gains and benefits to the environment. It will be more difficult to implement reforms that are economically costly (such as reforms that raise the costs of manufacturing in order to encourage conservation and recycling and those that impose higher fines against polluters), are likely to be unpopular (such as reforms that hike the price of water), or could undermine the Communist Party's authority (such as reforms that open up the media or give freer rein to civil society). But such measures are also necessary. And their high up-front costs must be weighed against the long-term costs to economic growth, public health, and social stability in which the Chinese government's continued inaction would result. The government must ensure greater accountability among local officials by promoting greater grass-roots oversight, greater transparency via the media or other outlets, and greater independence in the legal system.

China's leaders have shown themselves capable of bold reform in the past. Two and half decades ago, Deng Xiaoping and his supporters launched a set of ambitious reforms despite stiff political resistance and set the current economic miracle in motion. In order to continue on its extraordinary trajectory, China needs leaders with the vision to introduce a new set of economic and political initiatives that will transform the way the country does business. Without such measures, China will not return to global preeminence in the twenty-first century. Instead, it will suffer stagnation or regression—and all because leaders who recognized the challenge before them were unwilling to do what was necessary to surmount it.

Long Time Coming

The Prospects for Democracy in China

John L. Thornton

JANUARY/FEBRUARY 2008

China's leaders have held out the promise of some form of democracy to the people of China for nearly a century. After China's last dynasty, the Qing, collapsed in 1911, Sun Yat-sen suggested a three-year period of temporary military rule, followed by a six-year phase of "political tutelage," to guide the country's transition into a full constitutional republic. In 1940, Mao Zedong offered followers something he called "new democracy," in which leadership by the Communist Party would ensure the "democratic dictatorship" of the revolutionary groups over class enemies. And Deng Xiaoping, leading the country out of the anarchy of the Cultural Revolution, declared that democracy was a "major condition for emancipating the mind."

When they used the term "democracy," Sun, Mao, and Deng each had something quite different in mind. Sun's definition—which envisioned a constitutional government with universal suffrage, free elections, and separation of powers—came closest to a definition recognizable in the West. Through their deeds, Mao and Deng showed that despite their words, such

JOHN L. THORNTON is a Professor at Tsinghua University's School of Economics and Management and its School of Public Policy and Management, in Beijing, and Director of the university's Global Leadership Program. He is also Chair of the Board of the Brookings Institution.

concepts held little importance for them. Still, the three agreed that democracy was not an end in itself but rather a mechanism for achieving China's real purpose of becoming a country that could no longer be bullied by outside powers.

Democracy ultimately foundered under all three leaders. When Sun died, in 1925, warlordism and disunity still engulfed many parts of China. In his time, Mao showed less interest in democracy than in class struggle, mass movements, continuous revolution, and keeping his opponents off balance. And Deng demonstrated on a number of occasions—most dramatically in suppressing the Tiananmen protests of 1989—that he would not let popular democratic movements overtake party rule or upset his plan for national development.

Today, of course, China is not a democracy. The Chinese Communist Party (CCP) has a monopoly on political power, and the country lacks freedom of speech, an independent judiciary, and other fundamental attributes of a pluralistic liberal system. Many inside and outside China remain skeptical about the prospects for political reform. Yet much is happening—in the government, in the CCP, in the economy, and in society at large—that could change how Chinese think about democracy and shape China's political future.

Both in public and in private, China's leaders are once again talking about democracy, this time with increasing frequency and detail. (This article is based on conversations held over the past 14 months with a broad range of Chinese, including members of the CCP's Central Committee—the group of China's top 370 leaders—senior government officials, scholars, judges, lawyers, journalists, and leaders of nongovernmental organizations.) President Hu Jintao has called democracy "the common pursuit of mankind." During his 2006 visit to the United States, Hu went out of his way to broach the subject at each stop. And Premier Wen Jiabao, in his address to the 2007 National People's Congress, devoted to democracy and the rule of law more than twice the attention he had in any previous such speech. "Developing democracy and improving the legal system," Wen declared, "are basic requirements of the socialist system."

As with earlier leaders, what the present generation has in mind differs from the definition used in the West. Top officials stress that the CCP's leadership must be preserved. Although they see a role for elections, particularly at the local level, they assert that a "deliberative" form of politics that allows individual citizens and groups to add their views to the decision-making process is more appropriate for China than open, multiparty competition for national power. They often mention meritocracy, including the use of examinations to test candidates' competence for office, reflecting an age-old Chinese belief that the government should be made up of the country's most talented. Chinese leaders do not welcome the latitude of freedom of speech, press, or assembly taken for granted in the West. They say they support the orderly expansion of these rights but focus more on the group and social harmony—what they consider the common good.

Below the top tier of leaders (who usually speak from a common script), Chinese officials differ on whether "guided democracy" is where China's current political evolution will end or is a way station en route to a more standard liberal democratic model. East Asia provides examples of several possibilities: the decades-long domination of politics by the Liberal Democratic Party in Japan, the prosperity with limited press freedom of Singapore, and the freewheeling multiparty system of South Korea. China might follow one of these paths, some speculate, or blaze its own.

In a meeting in late 2006 with a delegation from the Brookings Institution (of which I was a member), Premier Wen was asked what he and other Chinese leaders meant by the word "democracy," what form democracy was likely to take in China, and over what time frame. "When we talk about democracy," Wen replied, "we usually refer to three key components: elections, judicial independence, and supervision based on checks and balances." Regarding the first, he could foresee direct and indirect elections expanding gradually from villages to towns, counties, and even provinces. He did not mention developments beyond this, however. As for China's judicial system, which is riddled with corruption, Wen stressed the need for reform to assure the judiciary's "dignity, justice, and independence." And he explained that "supervision"—a Chinese term for ensuring effective oversight—was necessary to restrain abuses of official power. He called for checks and balances within the CCP and for greater official accountability to the public. The media and China's nearly 200 million Internet users should also participate "as appropriate" in the supervision of the government's work, he observed. Wen's bottom line: "We have to move toward democracy. We have many problems, but we know the direction in which we are going."

FREE TO CHOOSE

Given the gap between the democratic aspirations professed by leaders such as Hu and Wen and the skepticism that their words elicit in the West, a better understanding is needed of where exactly the process of democratization stands in China today. Chinese citizens do not have the right to choose their national leaders, but for more than a decade, peasants across the country have held ballots to elect village chiefs. What is happening in the vast space between the farm and Zhongnanhai, the CCP's leadership compound in Beijing? Some answers can be gleaned by examining the three pillars of Wen's definition: elections, judicial independence, and supervision.

The Chinese constitution calls for a combination of direct and indirect polls to choose government leaders. In practice, competitive popular elections occur widely only in the country's 700,000 villages. With over 700 million farmers living in these villages, this is not an insignificant phenomenon, but the details tell a complex and at times contradictory story.

The original impulse behind village elections, which began in the early 1980s, was to promote competent local leaders who would grow the rural economy and implement national priorities such as the one-child policy. With the abandonment of collectivization at the end of the Cultural Revolution, a power vacuum emerged in the countryside. By most accounts, at first elections enjoyed the central government's active support and were generally conducted fairly. But in the early 1990s, authorities were reportedly taken aback by figures showing that only 40 percent of elected village chiefs were CCP members. Beijing eventually instructed local officials to ensure that the "leading role" of the Communist Party was maintained. Today, the majority of village chiefs are again party members, although the size of that majority can vary widely by region. Over 90 percent of the village heads in the provinces of Guangdong, Hubei, and Shandong belong to the party, but the figure drops to 60–70 percent in Fujian and Zhejiang. And even these figures overstate the actual percentage of village chiefs who were elected as party members: when nonparty candidates are elected, the CCP nearly always recruits them so as to ensure that it remains in charge while giving farmers the leaders they want.

Village elections have serious problems, including nepotism, vote buying, and the selection of incompetent or corrupt leaders. Proponents nonetheless maintain that the polls serve as a grass-roots training ground for democratic habits. In fact, the most fervent opponents of village elections in China tend to be the township officials whose own jobs would be in danger if the central government decided to expand direct voting to the next level up.

Some of the more intriguing electoral experiments in China

over the past decade have in fact taken place in townships. Burdened with administering the numerous social programs and benefits on which many citizens depend, township governments are often the focus of antigovernment sentiment and social unrest. Effective leadership there is thus critical to preserving social stability, a top priority for Chinese leaders. A few competitive township polls took place as early as 1995–96; the boldest experiment occurred in 1998 in Buyun, in a remote corner of Sichuan. The local Buyun government conducted a competitive, direct election in which some 6,000 eligible adults cast votes. The process received wide media coverage inside China and was criticized in the official press for violating the constitution, which grants the local People's Congress authority to choose the township leader. But to the surprise of many, the central government neither approved the Buyun results nor nullified them, and the elected mayor, Tan Xiaoqiu, remained in office. In 2001, the CCP Central Committee reaffirmed that directly electing a township head was unconstitutional. Buyun responded by tweaking its election process to bring it in line with the letter of the law but not its spirit: in the next election, citizens elected a candidate for township head, who was then recommended by the local party committee and elected unopposed by the People's Congress.

Perhaps in part due to Buyun's legal troubles, most townships that have experimented with elections have chosen the less radical model called the "open recommendation and selection" system, under which any adult resident can run for township head, a council of community leaders then narrows the candidate pool to two finalists, and the local People's Congress makes the final selection. This is not a direct ballot but a way of introducing a measure of competition and transparency in the selection of local leaders. By 2001–2, there was some form of competitive ballot in almost 2,000 township elections, five percent of the national total.

The significance of township elections should not be overstated. Townships are at the lowest administrative rung in the Chinese government structure, and even election supporters acknowledge that the process is still in its infancy. Nonetheless, when conducted successfully, such electoral experiments can give township leaders a degree of popular legitimacy. They introduce competition among cadres and, to a lesser extent, between party and nonparty members where absolutely none existed before. The expectation is that competition, even if controlled, will raise the quality of governance. Some Chinese scholars also find it notable that some township heads are conducting themselves with greater confidence because they know they enjoy a popular mandate and are therefore more willing to challenge the local party secretaries. This can create headaches for the CCP, one central government researcher noted, but it may also be the first seed of a culture of checks and balances.

Authorities in Beijing, for their part, are closely watching the experiments. In an echo of the dynamic that initiated market reforms in the 1980s, the center now encourages governance experimentation at the local level, albeit within boundaries. A senior official at the Central Party School told me, for instance, that in the prosperous province of Jiangsu, a pilot program would soon have all of the townships conducting competitive polls. As different localities try different things, he said, the Central Party School will study the results.

Electoral experiments at the county level—one administrative rung up from a township—have also attracted attention. Since 2000, 11 counties in Hubei and Jiangsu have conducted "open recommendation and selection" polls for the position of county deputy chief. This represents less than half a percent of the counties and county-level cities nationwide, but any reform of leadership selection in counties, which have an average population of about 450,000 each, would be significant news.

Limited experimentation has also occurred in urban areas.

In 2003, 12 private citizens stood as independent candidates for district People's Congresses in the city of Shenzhen, with two of them winning seats. A handful of independent candidates have also run for the People's Congress of the Haidian district in Beijing, home to China's top universities. Almost all independent candidates for people's congresses fail in their bids, yet the number of such candidates is exploding: from fewer than 100 nationwide in 2003 to more than 40,000 in 2006–7, according to Li Fan, a former government official who is now a leading election-reform advocate. Li predicts that the number of independent candidates will reach the hundreds of thousands in 2011–12 and thinks popular demand for political participation will continue to grow as Chinese society diversifies and opens up.

In recent years, China's leaders have also made an effort to expand competitive selection within the CCP. Some experts believe that the development of "intraparty democracy" is even more significant for China's long-term political reform than the experiments in local governance. They consider a CCP that accepts open debate, internal leadership elections, and decision-making by ballot to be a prerequisite for democracy in the country as a whole. President Hu and Premier Wen routinely call for more discussion, consultation, and group decision-making within the CCP. Intraparty democracy was a centerpiece of Hu's keynote address to the CCP's 17th Party Congress last fall. Not long after the meeting, Li Yuanchao, the newly appointed head of the Party Organization Department, published a 7,000-character essay in the *People's Daily* elaborating on Hu's call for further reform in the party. The fact that Hu himself does not wield the personal authority of Mao, Deng, or his predecessor, Jiang Zemin, and relies on consensus within the nine-member Politburo Standing Committee, is itself noted as progress in unwinding the overcentralization of power at the national level.

One of the ways the CCP has begun to introduce intraparty democracy is by putting forward multiple candidates for positions. Fifteen percent of the nominees for the 17th Party Congress were rejected in party ballots. In the 2006–7 national election cycle, the official media reported, 296 townships in 16 provinces chose local party leaders through direct voting by party members as part of a pilot project. In a handful of localities, one government scholar told me, county party secretaries were also being elected through a direct vote.

If intraparty democracy takes hold, some scholars predict a trend in which like-minded cadres will coalesce to form more distinct interest groups within the CCP. A senior official of the Central Party School told our Brookings delegation that "interest groups" were no longer taboo within the party, although organized "factions" were not permitted. Still, some analysts predict that the CCP may one day resemble Japan's ruling Liberal Democratic Party, within which formal, organized factions compete for senior political slots and advocate different policy positions.

In a major speech at the Central Party School in June last year, Hu exhorted the CCP's top leadership to "perfect the intraparty democratic system and bring into full play the party's creative vigor." Then, seemingly in a demonstration of the very intraparty democracy Hu was advocating, a nonbinding straw poll was conducted among the several hundred senior leaders present to gauge their preferences for candidates to the next Politburo and its Standing Committee—in other words, for who should rule China over the next five years.

Some Chinese analysts believe that Hu, in his remarks at the Central Party School, may have been foreshadowing a new policy approach. "Emancipating the mind, an essential requirement of the party's ideological line and a magic weapon of ours in dealing with all kind[s] of new situation[s] and problems lying on the road ahead of us and in our continuous efforts to create a new phase in our cause, must be upheld firmly," Hu told his audience. In asking his colleagues to unshackle themselves from rigid thinking, he was understood to be encouraging them to be more pragmatic in their thinking as China evolves politically. More specifically, Hu was thought to be both indicating to orthodox party thinkers that Mao's was not the only way to define "democracy" and signaling to more reform-minded members of the Central Committee that simply copying Western models was not necessarily the answer either.

THE RULE OF LAW

Of Wen's three pillars of democracy—elections, judicial independence, and supervision—judicial independence is in some ways the most striking. The question of whether the CCP serves the law or vice versa has always made judicial independence a delicate subject in China.

The Chinese judicial system has made great strides over the past three decades, but it still has far to go. In 1980, when the judicial system was just starting to rebuild itself after the devastation of the Cultural Revolution, Chinese courts nationwide accepted a total of 800,000 cases. By 2006, that number had jumped tenfold, reflecting the transformation of the place of law in society. China has passed over 250 new laws in the past 30 years and is in the midst of creating an entire national code from nothing.

Until the mid-1980s, the majority of Chinese judges and prosecutors were former military personnel with little formal education of any sort, let alone legal training. Judicial independence was not the goal of such a system; if anything, it was something to be guarded against. Unsurprisingly, given that the purpose of the courts was to carry out the party line, judges and prosecutors were highly ideological. But starting in the mid-1980s, university graduates were assigned by the state to become judges and prosecutors. By the late 1990s, a master's degree in law was considered an unwritten prerequisite to becoming a senior judge.

Paralleling the rise in the quality of judges and prosecutors has been the change in the status of China's lawyers. Before the late 1980s, all lawyers were employees of the state; private practice did not exist. The first "cooperative law firms" appeared in 1988–89, and today China has 118,000 licensed lawyers practicing in 12,000 firms. (To compare, the United States has more than eight times as many lawyers for a population one-fourth the size of China's.) The growth of private practice has propelled the further professionalization of the system as a whole, partly because lawyers need to win cases (or at least lighter sentences) for their clients in order to prosper. Prosecutors still win over 90 percent of their cases, but as the quality of lawyers has improved and arguments have grown more intricate, prosecutors—and judges—have had to improve their own competence. Party bosses still interfere in the judicial process, and the central government still decides politically sensitive cases, but most observers agree that with disputes becoming more complex, the frequency and degree of such interference are declining.

China has adopted a number of major statutes intended to protect citizens from government wrongdoing. The Public Servants Law of 2005 sets a high standard for conduct by officials. The State Compensation Law of 1994 is meant to make amends for government failures. Perhaps most significant, the Administrative Litigation Law, adopted in 1989, enables citizens to sue the state; some 13,000 suits were filed in the law's first year. Today, more than 150,000 cases are filed annually against the government, and several successful ones have been hailed in the media.

Still, Chinese officials acknowledge that the judicial process remains rife with problems. One of the most serious obstacles to impartial verdicts is the web of personal relationships known as guanxi—bonds forged over years by the exchange of favors and assistance—on which so many decisions in China are based. These ties can have an especially constraining effect on prosecutorial and court decisions. Judges in China routinely talk to the parties in a case privately, creating situations in which *guanxi* and corruption can readily contaminate the process. Some experts have suggested raising judges' salaries and taking other steps to create a judicial elite distinct from other government officials in order to address this endemic weakness.

China's main challenge is no longer the lack of a comprehensive legal code but the chasm between what is on the books and its implementation, especially at the local level and in politically sensitive cases. Rights guaranteed by the landmark Criminal Procedure Law of 1996, such as timely access to counsel and exculpatory evidence, are often denied or simply ignored. A small but growing group of private lawyers—sometimes referred to as "rights defenders"—take on sensitive cases and unjust prosecutions, in part to highlight instances in which the judicial system itself violates the law. Although they rarely win and are sometimes themselves harassed or even jailed, these activist lawyers believe that insistently pointing out the discrepancy between the official goal of a fair judicial system and the reality on the ground can over time narrow the gap.

Another major obstacle is the sway that local officials continue to hold over the courts. Local CCP committees are integrally involved in the appointment of judges and prosecutors, and local governments have discretion over salaries and budgets throughout the judicial system. The situation shares some similarities with the Chinese banking system a decade ago, when the influence of local officials over bank branches resulted in a vast pool of so-called policy loans. The explosion in nonperforming debt eventually forced Beijing to spend $60 billion from central government coffers to bail out the banks, after which then Premier Zhu Rongji pushed through a reorganization that transferred final authority over personnel and loan decisions to the banks' headquarters. Banking reform may offer a promising model for the restructuring that the judicial system needs.

According to the 1999 amendment to the constitution, China is now officially a "country governed according to law." But the CCP, not the government, holds ultimate power. An increasing number of scholars argue that what the country needs, therefore, is a party and party members who unambiguously understand that they are not above the law. One proponent of this view, Professor Zhuo Zeyuan, of the Central Party School, last year gave a two-hour talk on his ideas to all 24 members of the Politburo. A Central Party School leader told me later that the proper relationship between the ruling party and the constitution was unambiguous: the CCP should be governed by the law. As with so many things in China today, the rub is the gap between theory and practice.

The CCP firmly maintains the levers that control the courts and manipulates them when necessary. In addition, it operates a separate, parallel system for dealing with errant party members that includes the use of detention and interrogation and in some cases is more draconian than the regular legal system. Recently, there have been signs that the party may be starting to see the need for more due process in its practices. Professor Jerome Cohen, of New York University Law School, one of the West's foremost experts on the Chinese legal system, has noted that local party organizations in at least 20 provinces have established a disciplinary system for CCP members that includes guarantees such as a notice of alleged wrongdoing, the opportunity to defend oneself against charges (including the right to call supporting witnesses), a statement of reasons for a final decision, and an opportunity to appeal. Some of these rights have long been in the CCP charter but were never implemented seriously.

Chinese leaders appear to realize that the China of 2008 is far too complex to be ruled entirely by fiat from Beijing and has to be governed by laws through a competent legal system enjoying the public's confidence. Lack of faith in the courts is one reason people take to the streets, and official figures show that tens of thousands of public protests occur in China each year. It is not surprising then that leaders such as Premier Wen want the party and the state to stop interfering in routine judicial matters. But the leadership still insists on controlling sensitive cases and the judicial system at the macro level. The question is whether the CCP can succeed in building a fair and independent judicial system while maintaining control at the very top.

OVERSIGHT

The Chinese system does not lack for institutions meant to keep officials honest. The oldest of these is the traditional petition system, dating to the imperial era, which allows people to take their grievances directly to higher authorities. Each ministry in Beijing has an office that handles such complaints. But the petition is seen as a last resort, and few cases are satisfactorily resolved: the process is opaque and depends on the goodwill of the anonymous officials evaluating the appeals.

Another oversight institution, the CCP's Central Commission for Discipline Inspection, staffed by eight deputies and 120 senior members and headed by a Politburo Standing Committee member, is charged with fighting corruption and other misconduct by party members. Its counterparts on the government side are the Ministry of Supervision and the Anti-Corruption Bureau of the Supreme People's Procuratorate, responsible for prosecuting errant government officials. One of the functions of the official Xinhua News Agency, finally, is to gather information on corruption nationwide and produce internal reports for the central leadership.

Yet despite these multiple mechanisms, the problem of official corruption remains serious, and leaders routinely cite moral turpitude as one of the party's main challenges. As the economy has surged for more than two decades, so have opportunities for graft. High-profile cases such as that of Zheng Xiaoyu, the former head of the State Food and Drug Administration executed this past July for taking bribes from pharmaceutical companies, feed the perception of endemic rot. According to the CCP, over 97,000 officials were disciplined in 2006, of whom 80 percent were guilty of dereliction of duty, taking bribes, or violating financial regulations. "The formal [supervision] system on the whole has failed," one government researcher told me. At lower levels, a basic structural flaw in the supervision system mirrors that of the courts: the heads of the discipline inspection commissions are appointed by local leaders, who predictably tend to select relatives, friends, protégés, or colleagues. It was only in 2006 that a rule was implemented requiring that commission heads at the provincial level be appointed by the central government.

President Hu and Premier Wen face a basic dilemma. They know that rooting out corruption, which makes citizens cynical about one-party rule, must be their top governance priority. But they must act while maintaining the loyalty of local officials, through whom the CCP governs the country. To augment the formal mechanisms of supervision, the government is increasingly turning to alternative channels. In Beijing, some districts are using public opinion polling to gauge satisfaction with individual government offices, and Beijing's Urban Planning Commission has retained a consulting firm to help it take better account of public opinion in assessing redevelopment projects.

Another promising trend is the rapid commercialization of the Chinese press. The government still exercises extensive control over the media through government ownership of outlets and censorship. The redlines that journalists cannot cross still exist. But changes are taking place. As independent Chinese publications seek readers and advertisers, they pursue stories that people want to read; like their counterparts in the West, they have discovered that investigative journalism sells. In one widely discussed case, a veteran reporter for the *China Economic Times* wrote an in-depth account in 2002 of the Beijing taxi-licensing system. Due to alleged collusion between company owners and the government supervisory body, drivers were being forced to work shockingly long hours for low wages. The newspaper sold out almost immediately. The Central Propaganda Bureau responded by banning other publications from reporting on the story. The city's Transportation Bureau ordered drivers not to read the article. Some of the taxi drivers quoted in the article received death threats, and the author had to be protected by bodyguards for three months. The public uproar mounted, however, as the news spread to the Internet. Eight days after the story was printed, then Vice Premier Wen Jiabao issued an official statement supporting the taxi drivers and directing that a report on the situation be prepared for then Premier Zhu Rongji.

One experiment that has caught the attention of many Chinese is the government's decision to allow foreign journalists to travel and report freely throughout China (with the exception of Tibet) from January 2007 through the 2008 Beijing Olympics. "It's clearly a test," a Chinese newspaper editor said, "to see how the foreign press uses its new freedom. Unless something goes terribly wrong, it's hard to see how the government can reimpose the old system when the Olympics are over." Not surprisingly, there have been numerous teething problems: in July, several foreign journalists covering an antigovernment demonstration held by an international human rights group were detained for several hours. Still, foreign correspondents in Beijing report that, in general, restrictions on their movements and activities have been relaxed noticeably since the new policy was announced.

In the past several years, the Internet and cell phones have started to challenge traditional media by becoming channels for the expression of citizen outrage, at times forcing the government to take action. One celebrated instance was the "nail house" incident in the sprawling metropolis of Chongqing, in central China. For three years, a middle-class couple stubbornly refused to sell their house to property developers who, with the municipal government's permission, planned to raze the entire area and turn it into a commercial district. The neighbors had long ago moved away. The developer tried to intimidate the couple by digging a three-story canyon around their lone house, but the tactic backfired spectacularly. Photos of their home's precarious situation were posted on the Internet, sparking outrage among Chinese across the country. Within weeks, tens of thousands of messages had been posted lambasting the Chongqing government for letting such a thing happen. Reporters camped out at the site; even official newspapers took up the couple's cause. In the end, the couple settled for a new house and over $110,000 in compensation. The widely read daily *Beijing News* ran a commentary that would have been inconceivable in a Chinese newspaper a decade ago: "This is an inspiration for the Chinese public in the emerging age of civil rights. . . . Media coverage of this event has been rational and constructive. This is encouraging for the future of citizens defending their rights according to the law."

In another example of the marriage of new technology and citizen action, last May angry residents in the southern coastal city of Xiamen launched a campaign to force the city government to stop the construction of a large chemical plant on the outskirts of the city. Their weapon was the cell phone. In a matter of days, hundreds of thousands of text messages opposing the plant were forwarded, spreading like a virus throughout the country. Xiamen authorities, who had ignored popular opposition to the plant before, suddenly announced that construction would be suspended until an environmental impact study could be completed. Dissatisfied with this half measure, citizens again used message networking to organize a march of some 7,000 people to demand a permanent halt to the construction. Although local party newspapers blasted the protest as illegal, it was allowed to proceed without incident, marking one of the largest peaceful demonstrations in China in recent years.

DEMOCRACY IN CHINA

Recent progress in elections, judicial independence, and oversight is part of the transformation of Chinese society and the expansion of personal freedoms that have accompanied three decades of breakneck economic reform and development. The government remains intrusive in many areas but much less so than before.

In the past 20 years, several hundred million Chinese have migrated from the countryside to the cities—the largest wave of rapid urbanization in history. Until a decade ago, the government enforced stringent controls on internal migration. Today, officials cite the additional 300 million farmers expected to move to cities over the next two decades as a positive force that will help alleviate China's urban-rural income gap. The state once assigned jobs and housing to every urban resident. Now, urban Chinese enjoy overseas travel to study, work, or play. Ten years ago, a Chinese citizen needed to get permission from his supervisor, his work unit's party secretary, and the local police just to apply for a passport, a process that could take six months, assuming the passport was approved at all. The entire procedure takes less than a week today, and approval is nearly as automatic as it is in the United States. Less than two decades ago, all foreigners in Beijing were forced to live in designated locations, such as hotels or compounds guarded by military police. Today, foreigners and Chinese live side by side. When Chinese are asked about the democratization of their society, they are as likely to mention these sorts of changes as they are elections or judicial reform. They may be confusing the concept of liberty with that of democracy, but it would be a mistake to dismiss the expansion of their personal freedom as insignificant.

A senior Communist Party official I know marveled privately that ten years ago it would have been unimaginable for someone in his position to even be having an open discussion about democracy with an American. Now, the debate in China is no longer about whether to have democracy, he said, but about when and how. One thing the party should do immediately, he felt, was reform the National People's Congress so that it does not become a "retirement home" for former officials; the National People's Congress should be populated by competent professionals and eventually become a true legislative body. The government should also implement direct elections up to the provincial level, he argued, not Western-style multiparty elections but at least a contest involving a real choice of candidates.

The chair of one of China's largest corporations, who is also an alternate member of the CCP Central Committee, told me that better corporate governance in companies listed on overseas stock exchanges (and thus held to international norms), such as his, was another example of the expansion of "democratic habits" in China. Although corporate governance in China remains a work in progress, this chair said, the general trend among state-owned enterprises, especially those listed abroad, is toward greater transparency, stronger and more independent boards of directors, and management by mutually agreed rules. Over time, working in such an environment is likely to inculcate more democratic patterns of thinking in China's business elite, as well as in senior government officials who sit on the boards of state-owned enterprises.

Over the last century, no one has thought more about the

promise of democracy in their country or been more dismayed by its elusiveness than the Chinese themselves. Again and again, they have witnessed a native democratic impulse surge and crash or be crushed prematurely. The empress dowager Cixi quashed the 1898 "hundred days of reform" initiated by advisers to the emperor Guangxu. The optimism that surrounded Sun's inauguration as provisional president of the Chinese Republic on January 1, 1912, was soon extinguished by the military ruler Yuan Shikai, who tried to crown himself as the first emperor of a new dynasty in 1915. Progressives within both the Nationalist and the Communist Parties espoused democratic forms of government in the 1930s before the onslaught of wars with Japan and then with each other. The establishment of the People's Republic in 1949 augured an era of self-determination, prosperity, and democracy. But that hope was crushed under the foot of Mao's relentless political campaigns, culminating in the Cultural Revolution. Before the tragedy of Tiananmen in 1989, the 1980s were a period of intense political ferment, when democracy was debated inside the government, think tanks, universities, and intellectual salons.

Compared to in those periods, the way in which China's leaders talk about democracy today may seem cautious. Critics argue that this reflects the government's lack of real commitment to political reform. Optimists believe that gradualism will make the current liberalization last longer than the euphoric, but ultimately failed, experiences of the past. One of China's elder statesman—who has known personally all of the country's top leaders since Mao—insisted to me that democracy has always been the "common aspiration" of the Chinese people. They are determined to get it right, he argued, but they require patience from the West. "Please let the Chinese experiment," he said. "Let us explore."

Where that exploration will lead is an open question. There is a range of views among Chinese about how long will be required for democracy to take root, but there is also some agreement. One official put it this way: "No one predicts five years. Some think ten to 15. Some say 30 to 35. And no one says 60." Others predict that the process will take at least two more generational changes in the CCP's leadership—a scenario that would place its advent around the year 2022.

In 2004, a survey was conducted among nearly 700 local officials who had attended a provincial training program. More than 60 percent of the officials polled said that they were dissatisfied with the state of democracy in the country then, and 63 percent said that political reform in China was too slow. On the other hand, 59 percent of them said that economic development should take precedence over democracy. And tellingly, 67 percent of the cadres supported popular elections for village leaders and 41 percent supported elections for county heads, compared with only 13 percent for elections for provincial governors and just 9 percent for elections for China's president.

Some Chinese like to point out that it took the United States almost two centuries to achieve universal suffrage. In the first several American presidential elections, most states restricted voting to white male landowners—no more than ten percent of the adult U.S. population at the time. Women had to wait until the twentieth century, and blacks in effect until the 1960s. "This is one issue," a Beijing newspaper editor joked, "about which we Chinese may be less patient than you Americans."

Last spring, an article provocatively titled "Democracy Is a Good Thing" caused a small sensation in China. Published in a journal closely linked to the CCP, the article was authored by Yu Keping, the head of a think tank that reports directly to the CCP Central Committee. Although hardly blind to democracy's drawbacks (it "affords opportunities for certain sweet-talking political fraudsters to mislead the people"), Yu was forthright and specific in his approval of it: "Among all the political systems that have been invented and implemented, democracy is the one with the least number of flaws. That is to say, relatively speaking, democracy is the best political system for humankind."

Yu did not predict an easy road to democracy in China. "Under conditions of democratic rule," he observed, "officials must be elected by the citizens and they must gain the endorsement and support of the majority of the people; their powers will be curtailed by the citizens, they cannot do whatever they want, they have to sit down across from the people and negotiate. Just these two points alone already make many people dislike it. Therefore, democratic politics will not operate on its own; it requires the people themselves and the government officials who represent the interests of the people to promote and implement [it]."

Clearly, some people at the center of the Chinese system are thinking actively about these fundamental questions. The issue is whether and how these ideas will be translated into practice. China must now complete the transition begun in recent years, from a system that relies on the authority and judgment of one or a few dominating figures to a government run by commonly accepted and binding rules. The institutionalization of power is shared by all countries that have successfully made the transition to democracy. China's ongoing experiments with local elections, reform of the judicial system, and the strengthening of oversight are all part of the shift to a more rule-based system. So are the ways in which Chinese society continues to open and diversify, incrementally creating a civil society.

Institutionalization may progress the most over the next few years in an area that could be decisive in determining China's political evolution: leadership succession. How a country manages the transfer of power at the very top sends an unmistakable signal to all levels below. On this point, China has already come some way. To be chosen as Mao's successor was the most perilous position one could be put in. Deng had his own problems anointing a durable successor; he remained the most powerful man in China for nearly a decade after relinquishing all his official posts in 1989. It was his successor, Jiang, who saw the first peaceful transfer of power in modern Chinese history, when he gave up his positions to Hu. Jiang has remained a power behind the scenes, but no one would suggest that he holds the influence that Deng did.

One senior leader told me that the issue of succession can no longer be managed effectively in the ad hoc manner of the past. Both China and the world have changed too much; the process of selecting the country's leaders needs to be institutionalized. The problem, he explained, was that an acceptable new process has yet to be put in place, and until one is, it would be impractical to jettison the old system. China finds itself in an ambiguous transition at the moment. For his part, this leader believed that progress might be seen by the time of the Third Plenum of the 17th Party Congress, in 2009. Some party members have even suggested that Hu's heir as general secretary of the CCP could be chosen through a vote of the entire Central Committee when Hu retires in 2012. The method by which Hu's successor is selected will be an unmistakable indicator of the political future China's current generation of leaders envisions—signaling whether they believe, as Sun did a century ago, that democracy can best deliver the prosperity, independence, and liberty for which the Chinese people have struggled and sacrificed for so many years.

The Rise of China and the Future of the West

Can the Liberal System Survive?

G. John Ikenberry

JANUARY/FEBRUARY 2008

The rise of China will undoubtedly be one of the great dramas of the twenty-first century. China's extraordinary economic growth and active diplomacy are already transforming East Asia, and future decades will see even greater increases in Chinese power and influence. But exactly how this drama will play out is an open question. Will China overthrow the existing order or become a part of it? And what, if anything, can the United States do to maintain its position as China rises?

Some observers believe that the American era is coming to an end, as the Western-oriented world order is replaced by one increasingly dominated by the East. The historian Niall Ferguson has written that the bloody twentieth century witnessed "the descent of the West" and "a reorientation of the world" toward the East. Realists go on to note that as China gets more powerful and the United States' position erodes, two things are likely to happen: China will try to use its growing influence to

G. JOHN IKENBERRY is Albert G. Milbank Professor of Politics and International Affairs at Princeton University and the author of *After Victory: Institutions, Strategic Restraint, and the Rebuilding of Order After Major Wars.*

reshape the rules and institutions of the international system to better serve its interests, and other states in the system—especially the declining hegemon—will start to see China as a growing security threat. The result of these developments, they predict, will be tension, distrust, and conflict, the typical features of a power transition. In this view, the drama of China's rise will feature an increasingly powerful China and a declining United States locked in an epic battle over the rules and leadership of the international system. And as the world's largest country emerges not from within but outside the established post-World War II international order, it is a drama that will end with the grand ascendance of China and the onset of an Asian-centered world order.

That course, however, is not inevitable. The rise of China does not have to trigger a wrenching hegemonic transition. The U.S.-Chinese power transition can be very different from those of the past because China faces an international order that is fundamentally different from those that past rising states confronted. China does not just face the United States; it faces a Western-centered system that is open, integrated, and rule-based, with wide and deep political foundations. The nuclear revolution, meanwhile, has made war among great powers unlikely—eliminating the major tool that rising powers have used to overturn international systems defended by declining hegemonic states. Today's Western order, in short, is hard to overturn and easy to join.

This unusually durable and expansive order is itself the product of farsighted U.S. leadership. After World War II, the United States did not simply establish itself as the leading world power. It led in the creation of universal institutions that not only invited global membership but also brought democracies and market societies closer together. It built an order that facilitated the participation and integration of both established great powers and newly independent states. (It is often forgotten that this postwar order was designed in large part to reintegrate the defeated Axis states and the beleaguered Allied states into a unified international system.) Today, China can gain full access to and thrive within this system. And if it does, China will rise, but the Western order—if managed properly—will live on.

As it faces an ascendant China, the United States should remember that its leadership of the Western order allows it to shape the environment in which China will make critical strategic choices. If it wants to preserve this leadership, Washington must work to strengthen the rules and institutions that underpin that order—making it even easier to join and harder to overturn. U.S. grand strategy should be built around the motto "The road to the East runs through the West." It must sink the roots of this order as deeply as possible, giving China greater incentives for integration than for opposition and increasing the chances that the system will survive even after U.S. relative power has declined.

The United States' "unipolar moment" will inevitably end. If the defining struggle of the twenty-first century is between China and the United States, China will have the advantage. If the defining struggle is between China and a revived Western system, the West will triumph.

TRANSITIONAL ANXIETIES

China is well on its way to becoming a formidable global power. The size of its economy has quadrupled since the launch of market reforms in the late 1970s and, by some estimates, will double again over the next decade. It has become one of the world's major manufacturing centers and consumes roughly a third of the global supply of iron, steel, and coal. It has accumulated massive foreign reserves, worth more than $1 trillion at the end of 2006. China's military spending has increased at an inflation-adjusted rate of over 18 percent a year, and its diplomacy has extended its reach not just in Asia but also in Africa, Latin America, and the Middle East. Indeed, whereas the Soviet Union rivaled the United States as a military competitor only, China is emerging as both a military and an economic rival—heralding a profound shift in the distribution of global power.

Power transitions are a recurring problem in international relations. As scholars such as Paul Kennedy and Robert Gilpin have described it, world politics has been marked by a succession of powerful states rising up to organize the international system. A powerful state can create and enforce the rules and institutions of a stable global order in which to pursue its interests and security. But nothing lasts forever: long-term changes in the distribution of power give rise to new challenger states, who set off a struggle over the terms of that international order. Rising states want to translate their newly acquired power into greater authority in the global system—to reshape the rules and institutions in accordance with their own interests. Declining states, in turn, fear their loss of control and worry about the security implications of their weakened position.

These moments are fraught with danger. When a state occupies a commanding position in the international system, neither it nor weaker states have an incentive to change the existing order. But when the power of a challenger state grows and the power of the leading state weakens, a strategic rivalry ensues, and conflict—perhaps leading to war—becomes likely. The danger of power transitions is captured most dramatically in the case of late-nineteenth-century Germany. In 1870, the United Kingdom had a three-to-one advantage in economic power over Germany and a significant military advantage as well; by 1903, Germany had pulled ahead in terms of both economic and military power. As Germany unified and grew, so, too, did its dissatisfactions and demands, and as it grew more powerful, it increasingly appeared as a threat to other great powers in Europe, and security competition began. In the strategic realignments that followed, France, Russia, and the United Kingdom, formerly enemies, banded together to confront an emerging Germany. The result was a European war. Many observers see this dynamic emerging in U.S.-Chinese relations. "If China continues its impressive economic growth over the next few decades," the realist scholar John Mearsheimer has written, "the United States and China are likely to engage in an intense security competition with considerable potential for war."

But not all power transitions generate war or overturn the old order. In the early decades of the twentieth century, the United Kingdom ceded authority to the United States without great conflict or even a rupture in relations. From the late 1940s to the early 1990s, Japan's economy grew from the equivalent of five percent of U.S. GDP to the equivalent of over 60 percent of U.S. GDP, and yet Japan never challenged the existing international order.

Clearly, there are different types of power transitions. Some states have seen their economic and geopolitical power grow dramatically and have still accommodated themselves to the existing order. Others have risen up and sought to change it. Some power transitions have led to the breakdown of the old order and the establishment of a new international hierarchy. Others have brought about only limited adjustments in the regional and global system.

A variety of factors determine the way in which power transitions unfold. The nature of the rising state's regime and the degree of its dissatisfaction with the old order are critical: at the end of the nineteenth century, the United States, a liberal country an ocean away from Europe, was better able to embrace the British-centered international order than Germany was. But even more decisive is the character of the international order itself—for it is the nature of the international order that shapes a rising state's choice between challenging that order and integrating into it.

OPEN ORDER

The postwar Western order is historically unique. Any international order dominated by a powerful state is based on a mix of coercion and consent, but the U.S.-led order is distinctive in that it has been more liberal than imperial—and so unusually accessible, legitimate, and durable. Its rules and institutions are rooted in, and thus reinforced by, the evolving global forces of democracy and capitalism. It is expansive, with a wide and widening array of participants and stakeholders. It is capable of generating tremendous economic growth and power while also signaling restraint—all of which make it hard to overturn and easy to join.

It was the explicit intention of the Western order's architects in the 1940s to make that order integrative and expansive. Before the Cold War split the world into competing camps, Franklin Roosevelt sought to create a one-world system managed by cooperative great powers that would rebuild war-ravaged Europe, integrate the defeated states, and establish mechanisms for security cooperation and expansive economic growth. In fact, it was Roosevelt who urged—over the opposition of Winston Churchill—that China be included as a permanent member of the UN Security Council. The then Australian ambassador to the United States wrote in his diary after his first meeting with Roosevelt during the war, "He said that he had numerous discussions with Winston about China and that he felt that Winston was 40 years behind the times on China and he continually referred to the Chinese as 'Chinks' and 'Chinamen' and he felt that this was very dangerous. He wanted to keep China as a friend because in 40 or 50 years' time China might easily become a very powerful military nation."

Over the next half century, the United States used the system of rules and institutions it had built to good effect. West Germany was bound to its democratic Western European neighbors through the European Coal and Steel Community (and, later, the European Community) and to the United States through the Atlantic security pact; Japan was bound to the United States through an alliance partnership and expanding economic ties. The Bretton Woods meeting in 1944 laid down the monetary and trade rules that facilitated the opening and subsequent flourishing of the world economy—an astonishing achievement given the ravages of war and the competing interests of the great powers. Additional agreements between the United States, Western Europe, and Japan solidified the open and multilateral character of the postwar world economy. After the onset of the Cold War, the Marshall Plan in Europe and the 1951 security pact between the United States and Japan further integrated the defeated Axis powers into the Western order.

In the final days of the Cold War, this system once again proved remarkably successful. As the Soviet Union declined, the Western order offered a set of rules and institutions that provided Soviet leaders with both reassurances and points of access—effectively encouraging them to become a part of the system. Moreover, the shared leadership of the order ensured accommodation of the Soviet Union. As the Reagan administration pursued a hard-line policy toward Moscow, the Europeans pursued détente and engagement. For every hard-line "push," there was a moderating "pull," allowing Mikhail Gorbachev to pursue high-risk reforms. On the eve of German unification, the fact that a united Germany would be embedded in European and Atlantic institutions—rather than becoming an independent great power—helped reassure Gorbachev that neither German nor Western intentions were hostile. After the Cold War, the Western order once again managed the integration of a new wave of countries, this time from the formerly communist world. Three particular features of the Western order have been critical to this success and longevity.

First, unlike the imperial systems of the past, the Western order is built around rules and norms of nondiscrimination and market openness, creating conditions for rising states to advance their expanding economic and political goals within it. Across history, international orders have varied widely in terms of whether the material benefits that are generated accrue disproportionately to the leading state or are widely shared. In the Western system, the barriers to economic participation are low, and the potential benefits are high. China has already discovered the massive economic returns that are possible by operating within this open-market system.

Second is the coalition-based character of its leadership. Past orders have tended to be dominated by one state. The stakeholders of the current Western order include a coalition of powers arrayed around the United States—an important distinction. These leading states, most of them advanced liberal democracies, do not always agree, but they are engaged in a continuous process of give-and-take over economics, politics, and security. Power transitions are typically seen as being played out between two countries, a rising state and a declining hegemon, and the order falls as soon as the power balance shifts. But in the current order, the larger aggregation of democratic capitalist states—and the resulting accumulation of geopolitical power—shifts the balance in the order's favor.

Third, the postwar Western order has an unusually dense, encompassing, and broadly endorsed system of rules and institutions. Whatever its shortcomings, it is more open and rule-based than any previous order. State sovereignty and the rule of law are not just norms enshrined in the United Nations Charter. They are part of the deep operating logic of the order. To be sure, these norms are evolving, and the United States itself has historically been ambivalent about binding itself to international law and institutions—and at no time more so than today. But the overall system is dense with multilateral rules and institutions—global and regional, economic, political, and security-related. These represent one of the great breakthroughs of the postwar era. They have laid the basis for unprecedented levels of cooperation and shared authority over the global system.

The incentives these features create for China to integrate into the liberal international order are reinforced by the changed nature of the international economic environment—especially the new interdependence driven by technology. The most farsighted Chinese leaders understand that globalization has changed the game and that China accordingly needs strong, prosperous partners around the world. From the United States' perspective, a healthy Chinese economy is vital to the United States and the rest of the world. Technology and the global economic revolution have created a logic of economic relations that is different from the past—making the political and institutional logic of the current order all the more powerful.

ACCOMMODATING THE RISE

The most important benefit of these features today is that they give the Western order a remarkable capacity to accommodate rising powers. New entrants into the system have ways of gaining status and authority and opportunities to play a role in governing the order. The fact that the United States, China, and other great powers have nuclear weapons also limits the ability of a rising power to overturn the existing order. In the age of nuclear deterrence, great-power war is, thankfully, no longer a mechanism of historical change. War-driven change has been abolished as a historical process.

The Western order's strong framework of rules and institutions is already starting to facilitate Chinese integration. At first, China embraced certain rules and institutions for defensive purposes: protecting its sovereignty and economic interests while seeking to reassure other states of its peaceful intentions by getting involved in regional and global groupings. But as the scholar Marc Lanteigne argues, "What separates China from other states, and indeed previous global powers, is that not only is it 'growing up' within a milieu of international institutions far more developed than ever before, but more importantly, it is doing so while making active use of these institutions to promote the country's development of global power status." China, in short, is increasingly working within, rather than outside of, the Western order.

China is already a permanent member of the UN Security Council, a legacy of Roosevelt's determination to build the universal body around diverse great-power leadership. This gives China the same authority and advantages of "great-power exceptionalism" as the other permanent members. The existing global trading system is also valuable to China, and increasingly so. Chinese economic interests are quite congruent with the current global economic system—a system that is open and loosely institutionalized and that China has enthusiastically embraced and thrived in. State power today is ultimately based on sustained economic growth, and China is well aware that no major state can modernize without integrating into the globalized capitalist system; if a country wants to be a world power, it has no choice but to join the World Trade Organization (WTO). The road to global power, in effect, runs through the Western order and its multilateral economic institutions.

China not only needs continued access to the global capitalist system; it also wants the protections that the system's rules and institutions provide. The WTO's multilateral trade principles and dispute-settlement mechanisms, for example, offer China tools to defend against the threats of discrimination and protectionism that rising economic powers often confront. The evolution of China's policy suggests that Chinese leaders recognize these advantages: as Beijing's growing commitment to economic liberalization has increased the foreign investment and trade China has enjoyed, so has Beijing increasingly embraced global trade rules. It is possible that as China comes to champion the WTO, the support of the more mature Western economies for the WTO will wane. But it is more likely that both the rising and the declining countries will find value in the quasi-legal mechanisms that allow conflicts to be settled or at least diffused.

The existing international economic institutions also offer opportunities for new powers to rise up through their hierarchies. In the International Monetary Fund and the World Bank, governance is based on economic shares, which growing countries can translate into greater institutional voice. To be sure, the process of adjustment has been slow. The United States and Europe still dominate the IMF. Washington has a 17 percent voting share (down from 30 percent)—a controlling amount, because 85 percent approval is needed for action—and the European Union has a major say in the appointment of ten of the 24 members of the board. But there are growing pressures, notably the need for resources and the need to maintain relevance, that will likely persuade the Western states to admit China into the inner circle of these economic governance institutions. The IMF's existing shareholders, for example, see a bigger role for rising developing countries as necessary to renew the institution and get it through its current crisis of mission. At the IMF's meeting in Singapore in September 2006, they agreed on reforms that will give China, Mexico, South Korea, and Turkey a greater voice.

As China sheds its status as a developing country (and therefore as a client of these institutions), it will increasingly be able to act as a patron and stakeholder instead. Leadership in these organizations is not simply a reflection of economic size (the United States has retained its voting share in the IMF even as its economic weight has declined); nonetheless, incremental advancement within them will create important opportunities for China.

POWER SHIFT AND PEACEFUL CHANGE

Seen in this light, the rise of China need not lead to a volcanic struggle with the United States over global rules and leadership. The Western order has the potential to turn the coming power shift into a peaceful change on terms favorable to the United States. But that will only happen if the United States sets about strengthening the existing order. Today, with Washington pre-occupied with terrorism and war in the Middle East, rebuilding Western rules and institutions might to some seem to be of only marginal relevance. Many Bush administration officials have been outright hostile to the multilateral, rule-based system that the United States has shaped and led. Such hostility is foolish and dangerous. China will become powerful: it is already on the rise, and the United States' most powerful strategic weapon is the ability to decide what sort of international order will be in place to receive it.

The United States must reinvest in the Western order, reinforcing the features of that order that encourage engagement, integration, and restraint. The more this order binds together capitalist democratic states in deeply rooted institutions; the more open, consensual, and rule-based it is; and the more widely spread its benefits, the more likely it will be that rising powers can and will secure their interests through integration and accommodation rather than through war. And if the Western system offers rules and institutions that benefit the full range of states—rising and falling, weak and strong, emerging and mature—its dominance as an international order is all but certain.

The first thing the United States must do is reestablish itself as the foremost supporter of the global system of governance that underpins the Western order. Doing so will first of all facilitate the kind of collective problem solving that makes all countries better off. At the same time, when other countries see the United States using its power to strengthen existing rules and institutions, that power is rendered more legitimate—and U.S. authority is strengthened. Countries within the West become more inclined to work with, rather than resist, U.S. power, which reinforces the centrality and dominance of the West itself.

Renewing Western rules and institutions will require, among other things, updating the old bargains that underpinned key postwar security pacts. The strategic understanding behind both NATO and Washington's East Asian alliances is that the United States will work with its allies to provide security and bring them in on decisions over the use of force, and U.S. allies, in return, will operate within the U.S.-led Western order. Security cooperation in the West remains extensive today, but with the main security threats less obvious than they were during the Cold War, the purposes and responsibilities of these alliances are under dispute. Accordingly, the United States needs to reaffirm the political value of these alliances—recognizing that they are part of a wider Western institutional architecture that allows states to do business with one another.

The United States should also renew its support for wide-ranging multilateral institutions. On the economic front, this would include building on the agreements and architecture of the WTO, including pursuing efforts to conclude the current Doha Round of trade talks, which seeks to extend market opportunities and trade liberalization to developing countries. The WTO is at a critical stage. The basic standard of nondiscrimination is at risk thanks to the proliferation of bilateral and regional trade agreements. Meanwhile, there are growing doubts over whether the WTO can in fact carry out trade liberalization, particularly in agriculture, that benefits developing countries. These issues may seem narrow, but the fundamental character of the liberal international order—its commitment to universal rules of openness that spread gains widely—is at stake. Similar doubts haunt a host of other multilateral agreements—on global warming and nuclear nonproliferation, among others—and they thus also demand renewed U.S. leadership.

The strategy here is not simply to ensure that the Western order is open and rule-based. It is also to make sure that the order does not fragment into an array of bilateral and "minilateral" arrangements, causing the United States to find itself tied to only a few key states in various regions. Under such a scenario, China would have an opportunity to build its own set of bilateral and "minilateral" pacts. As a result, the world would be broken into competing U.S. and Chinese spheres. The more security and economic relations are multilateral and all-encompassing, the more the global system retains its coherence.

In addition to maintaining the openness and durability of the order, the United States must redouble its efforts to integrate rising developing countries into key global institutions. Bringing emerging countries into the governance of the international order will give it new life. The United States and Europe must find room at the table not only for China but also for countries such as Brazil, India, and South Africa. A Goldman Sachs report on the so-called BRICs (Brazil, Russia, India, and China) noted that by 2050 these countries' economies could together be larger than those of the original G-6 countries (Germany, France, Italy, Japan, the United Kingdom, and the United States) combined. Each international institution presents its own challenges. The UN Security Council is perhaps the hardest to deal with, but its reform would also bring the greatest returns. Less formal bodies—the so-called G-20 and various other intergovernmental networks—can provide alternative avenues for voice and representation.

G. John Ikenberry

THE TRIUMPH OF THE LIBERAL ORDER

The key thing for U.S. leaders to remember is that it may be possible for China to overtake the United States alone, but it is much less likely that China will ever manage to overtake the Western order. In terms of economic weight, for example, China will surpass the United States as the largest state in the global system sometime around 2020. (Because of its population, China needs a level of productivity only one-fifth that of the United States to become the world's biggest economy.) But when the economic capacity of the Western system as a whole is considered, China's economic advances look much less significant; the Chinese economy will be much smaller than the combined economies of the Organization for Economic Cooperation and Development far into the future. This is even truer of military might: China cannot hope to come anywhere close to total OECD military expenditures anytime soon. The capitalist democratic world is a powerful constituency for the preservation—and, indeed, extension—of the existing international order. If China intends to rise up and challenge the existing order, it has a much more daunting task than simply confronting the United States.

The "unipolar moment" will eventually pass. U.S. dominance will eventually end. U.S. grand strategy, accordingly, should be driven by one key question: What kind of international order would the United States like to see in place when it is less powerful?

This might be called the neo-Rawlsian question of the current era. The political philosopher John Rawls argued that political institutions should be conceived behind a "veil of ignorance"— that is, the architects should design institutions as if they do not know precisely where they will be within a socioeconomic system. The result would be a system that safeguards a person's interests regardless of whether he is rich or poor, weak or strong.

The United States needs to take that approach to its leadership of the international order today. It must put in place institutions and fortify rules that will safeguard its interests regardless of where exactly in the hierarchy it is or how exactly power is distributed in 10, 50, or 100 years.

Fortunately, such an order is in place already. The task now is to make it so expansive and so institutionalized that China has no choice but to become a full-fledged member of it. The United States cannot thwart China's rise, but it can help ensure that China's power is exercised within the rules and institutions that the United States and its partners have crafted over the last century, rules and institutions that can protect the interests of all states in the more crowded world of the future. The United States' global position may be weakening, but the international system the United States leads can remain the dominant order of the twenty-first century.

A Partnership of Equals

How Washington Should Respond to China's Economic Challenge

C. Fred Bergsten

JULY/AUGUST 2008

To be an economic superpower, a country must be sufficiently large, dynamic, and globally integrated to have a major impact on the world economy. Three political entities currently qualify: the United States, the European Union, and China. Inducing China to become a responsible pillar of the global economic system (as the other two are) will be one of the great challenges of coming decades—particularly since at the moment China seems uninterested in playing such a role.

The United States remains the world's largest national economy, the issuer of its key currency, and in most years the leading source and recipient of foreign investment. The EU now has an even larger economy and even greater trade flows with the outside world, and the euro increasingly competes with the dollar as a global currency. China, the newest member of the club, is smaller than the other two but is growing more quickly and is more deeply integrated into the global economy.

C. FRED BERGSTEN is Director of the Peterson Institute for International Economics. This essay is adapted from his forthcoming, co-authored book, *China's Rise: Challenges and Opportunities* (Peterson Institute and the Center for Strategic and International Studies, 2008).

Its dramatic expansion is therefore having a powerful effect on the rest of the world. (China is often paired with India in such discussions, but India's GDP is less than half of China's. The value of the annual growth of China's trade exceeds the total annual value of India's trade. China will dominate its Asian neighbor for the foreseeable future.)

China poses a unique challenge because it is still poor, significantly nonmarketized, and authoritarian. All three characteristics reduce the likelihood that it will easily accept the systemic responsibilities that should ideally accompany superpower status. The integration of China into the existing global economic order will thus be more difficult than was, say, the integration of Japan a generation ago. The United States and the EU would like to co-opt China by integrating it into the regime that they have built and defended over the last several decades. There are increasing signs, however, that China has a different objective. In numerous areas, it is pursuing strategies that conflict with existing norms, rules, and institutional arrangements.

Some take this lightly, viewing it as simply the usual free-riding and skirting of responsibility by a powerful newcomer cleverly exploiting the loopholes and weak enforcement of existing international rules to pursue its perceived national interests. After all, they say, even the United States and the EU do the same on occasion, as do other major emerging-market economies. And to be sure, there is no evidence that China's challenges to the current economic order derive from any cohesive or comprehensive strategy concocted by the country's political or intellectual leadership. Despite calls in Beijing for "a new international economic order" and talk of how a "Beijing consensus" might supplant the so-called Washington consensus, to date China's proposed alternative approaches do not add up to a revisionist challenge to the status quo.

Nevertheless, the situation is worrisome. Given its status as a powerful newcomer benefiting from an efficient economic order, China actually has a profound interest in seeing that the international rules and institutions function effectively. It should be trying to strengthen the system, whether the present version or an alternative version more to its liking.

Moreover, Chinese recalcitrance seems to be increasing rather than decreasing over time. At the outset of its economic reform process, in the late 1970s, China was eager to join (and to replace Taiwan in) the International Monetary Fund (IMF) and the World Bank. These institutional ties subsequently played important, and apparently welcome, roles in China's early development success. Later, Beijing not only endured lengthy negotiations and an ever-expanding set of requirements in order to join the World Trade Organization (WTO) but also used the pro-market rules of that institution to overcome resistance to reform among die-hards inside China itself.

But a country's attitudes can change dramatically along with its circumstances. Russia, for example, was a supplicant for international capital and support after its bankruptcy in 1998 and with world oil prices near $20 a barrel, but it is aggressively pursuing a resumption of great-power status now that it has recovered and with oil over $100 a barrel. China appears to be undergoing a similar evolution, albeit with a more cautious leadership and an incremental style. It is also experiencing the same internal backlash against globalization as have the United States and many other countries. This attitudinal shift simply has to be reversed, even if doing so requires a fundamental adjustment of the international economic architecture.

TOWARD AN ASIAN BLOC?

On trade, China has been playing at best a passive and at worst a disruptive role. It makes no effort to hide its current preference for low-quality, politically motivated bilateral and regional trade arrangements rather than economically meaningful (and demanding) multilateral trade liberalization through the WTO. Since China is the world's largest surplus country and second-largest exporter, this poses two important challenges to the existing global regime.

First, China's refusal to contribute positively to the Doha Round of international trade negotiations has all but ensured the talks' failure. Beijing has declared that it should have no liberalization obligations whatsoever and has invented a new category of WTO membership ("recently acceded members") to justify its recalcitrance. Such a stance by a major trading power is akin to abstention and has practically guaranteed that the Doha negotiations will go nowhere. And since the global trading system does not stay in place, but is always moving either forward or backward, a collapse of the Doha Round would be quite serious: it would represent the first failure of a major multilateral trade negotiation in the postwar period and place the entire WTO system in jeopardy. China is not the only culprit in the Doha drama, of course. The United States and the EU have been unwilling to abandon their agricultural protectionism, other important emerging economies have been unwilling to meaningfully open their markets, and several poor countries have resisted contributing to a global package of reforms. But China, with its major stake in open trade, exhibits the sharpest contrast of all the major players between its objective interests and its revealed policy.

Second, China's pursuit of bilateral and regional trade agreements with neighboring countries is more about politics than economics. Its "free-trade agreement" with the Association of Southeast Asian Nations (ASEAN), for example, covers only a small share of its commerce with the countries in question; it is simply an effort to calm their fears of being swamped by their huge neighbor. Again, it is true that the United States and other major trading powers also factor foreign policy considerations into their selections of partners for regional and bilateral trade agreements. But they also insist on economic standards that largely conform to the WTO's rules. China is able to escape legal application of those rules by continuing to declare itself a "developing country" and by taking advantage of "special and differential treatment." But for a major global trading power to hide behind such loopholes provokes substantial international strains.

China is also hurting the global trading system by supporting the creation of a loose but potent Asian trading bloc. The network of regional agreements that started with one between China and ASEAN has steadily expanded to include virtually all other possible Asian permutations: parallel Japanese-ASEAN and South Korean-ASEAN deals; various bilateral partnerships, including perhaps a Chinese-Indian one; a "10 + 3" arrangement that brings together the ten ASEAN countries and all three Northeast Asian countries, and possibly even a "10 + 6" agreement that would broaden the group to include Australia, India, and New Zealand. All this activity is likely to produce, within the next decade, an East Asian free-trade area led by China.

Such a regional grouping would almost certainly trigger a sharp backlash from the United States and the EU, as well as from numerous developing countries, because of its new discrimination against them. Even more important, it would create a tripolar global economic regime—a configuration that could threaten existing global arrangements and multilateral cooperation.

China's challenges to the global trading system are most visible in its opposition to the U.S. proposal, launched at the Asia-Pacific Economic Cooperation forum in 2006, for a free-trade area of the Asia-Pacific. The APEC initiative, immediately endorsed by a number of those smaller member economies that fervently want to prevent trade conflict between the group's two superpowers, seeks to head off the looming confrontation between an Asia-only trading bloc and the United States, which could draw a line down the middle of the Pacific. The initiative would eventually consolidate the many preferential pacts in the Asia-Pacific region and offer an economically meaningful Plan B for widespread trade liberalization if the Doha Round definitively fails. China has led the opposition to the idea, demonstrating its preference for bilateral deals with minimal economic content and its lack of interest in trying to defend the broader trading order.

TRASHING THE IMF?

China's challenge to the international monetary order, meanwhile, is at least as serious. Alone among the world's major economies, China has rejected the adoption of a flexible exchange-rate policy, which would promote adjustment of its balance-of-payments position and avoid a buildup of large imbalances. Under IMF rules, China has the right to peg its currency—but it does not have the right to intervene massively in the foreign exchange market, as it has for the past five years, to maintain a hugely undervalued yuan and thereby boost its international competitive position. This violates the most basic norms of the IMF's Articles of Agreement, which require members to "avoid manipulating exchange rates ... in order to prevent effective balance of payments adjustment or to gain unfair competitive advantage." It is also a violation of the IMF's implementing guidelines, which explicitly proscribe the use of "prolonged, large-scale one-way" interventions to maintain competitive undervaluation.

The results are unprecedented for a major trading country. China's current account surplus has reached 11–12 percent of its GDP. By next year, its annual global surplus could approach $500 billion, approximating the value of the U.S. current account deficit. Its hoard of foreign currency exceeds

$1.6 trillion and is by far the world's largest. These imbalances and the unprecedented flow of international funds that they require could trigger a crash of the dollar and a "hard landing" for the global economy, severely compounding the current global financial crisis.

Previous surplus countries, notably Germany in the 1960s and 1970s and Japan in the 1970s and 1980s, have also resisted making necessary and inevitable adjustments to their currency pegs. But no earlier imbalances have ever approached the current Chinese one in terms of its share of the country's GDP. Moreover, all of these countries eventually agreed to conform to the international rules.

To date, however, China has resisted all entreaties to alter its behavior. Its announced move to "a managed floating exchange rate based on market supply and demand" in July 2005 has still not produced any significant rise in the trade-weighted value of its currency, despite the recent acceleration of the yuan's appreciation against the dollar, nor has it prevented continued huge surpluses in China's external accounts. The number of interventions in the currency markets that China has undertaken to block faster appreciation of the yuan has at least doubled since that time.

China has actually questioned the basic concept of international cooperation in dealing with these problems, claiming that a country's exchange rate is "an issue of national sovereignty" (rather than a quintessentially international concern in which foreign parties have an equal interest). It has objected even to the IMF's consideration of the issue. Its actions have raised an implicit threat that it might promote the creation of an Asian Monetary Fund, further eroding the global role of the IMF, and may seek a regional or even global role for its national currency over the long term. These monetary steps intensify the challenge to the global trading system because large exchange-rate misalignments are a potent stimulus for protectionism in deficit countries, as indicated at present by the numerous bills in Congress to address the China currency issue with trade sanctions.

On energy (China will shortly become the world's largest consumer of energy), the challenge China poses is less frontal, but only because there exists no body of agreed global doctrine, rules, and institutions. There are at least two conflicting energy regimes, the (periodically effective) producer cartel embodied in the Organization of the Petroleum Exporting Countries and the (very loose and incomplete) consumer anticartel embodied in the International Energy Agency. China is creating problems for both with its drive to line up "secure sources of supply" through long-term contracts with selected producing countries. It is unwilling to rely solely, or even primarily, on market mechanisms, attempting to insure itself against both output interruptions by the producers and the market power of other large consumers.

Here, as elsewhere, China is hardly alone in its behavior. But as the driving force behind the single most important commodity market in the world, the country has a particular interest in (and responsibility for) forging systemic responses rather than trying to carve out exceptions and special privileges for itself. China appears to be either unaware of the abject failure of such strategies in the past or confident that its contemporary clout will suffice to sustain its contractual arrangements even in difficult periods, and it is pursuing such strategies with respect to other raw materials as well as oil and gas.

On foreign aid, China may have already become the largest national donor (depending on how "aid" is defined), and it is posing a direct challenge to prevailing norms by ignoring the types of conditionality that have evolved throughout the donor community over the past quarter century. Beijing rejects not only the social standards (on human rights, labor conditions, and the environment) that have become prevalent but also the basic economic standards (such as poverty alleviation and good governance) that virtually all bilateral and multilateral aid agencies now require as a matter of course. As with its trade and commodity pacts, China's "conditionality" on aid is almost wholly political: insistence that the recipient countries support China's positions on global issues, in the United Nations and elsewhere, and funnel their primary products to China as reliable suppliers.

NEW RULES OF THE GAME

What these policies demonstrate is that China's international mindset has not kept pace with its breathtaking economic ascent. China continues to act like a small country with little impact on the global system at large and therefore little responsibility for it. Such a lag in perceptions is not difficult to understand, particularly as it regards a conservative leadership still following Deng Xiaoping's directive to maintain a low international profile. The central thrust of contemporary Chinese foreign policy is not to assume a large role in the world but to avoid international entanglements that could disrupt the country's ability to focus on its huge domestic challenges. Moreover, the speed at which China has risen is difficult for even the most experienced observers to comprehend. (The pattern is similar to the one that accompanied Japan's growth from the early 1970s into the 1980s, when its meteoric rise also triggered sharp global reactions, while Tokyo maintained a passive and reactive stance on almost all international issues.)

Even the strongest defenders of the current world trading system would concede that at least some of China's criticisms are valid. At best, the Doha Round will achieve only marginal liberalization of world trade after almost a decade of effort. The IMF has failed to enforce its own rules and is being forced to downsize. The World Bank has lost any clear direction. The G-7 (the group of highly industrialized states) has adopted a mutual nonaggression pact among its members, making its criticisms of outsiders such as China seem hypocritical. And by failing to adapt their governance structures to the dramatic changes in the relative economic power among nations, the international economic institutions have lost much of their legitimacy. The fact that some Chinese attitudes are understandable and some Chinese concerns legitimate does not lessen the significance of the challenge but rather suggests some of the logical components of an intelligent response.

To deal with the situation, Washington should make a subtle but basic change to its economic policy strategy toward Beijing. Instead of focusing on narrow bilateral problems, it should seek to develop a true partnership with Beijing so as to provide joint leadership of the global economic system. Only such a "G-2" approach will do justice, and be seen to do justice, to China's new role as a global economic superpower and hence as a legitimate architect and steward of the international economic order.

The present U.S. approach seeks to entice China to join the existing global economic order. Washington's fondness for the status quo is understandable given its basic success and the prominent role it accords Washington. But China is uncomfortable with the very notion of simply integrating into a system it had no role in developing. Both Chinese officials and Chinese scholars are actively discussing alternative structures for which China can be present at the creation. At one particularly contentious point in its negotiations to enter the WTO, the Chinese ambassador reportedly thundered, "We know we have to play the game your way now, but in ten years we will set the rules!" The existing system, moreover, has become increasingly sclerotic, and it might well be that the only way to overcome the enormous resistance to change (manifested in positions such as Europe's refusal to wind down its excessive quotas and give up some of its IMF executive-board seats) is to undertake a fundamental overhaul.

Current U.S. policy also purports to include tough enforcement measures to punish noncooperation: Washington has taken Beijing to the WTO for dispute settlement on a number of occasions and has tried to mobilize the IMF and the G-7 to penalize China for its undervalued currency. But Washington's criticism of Beijing has not been translated into any serious retaliatory pressure because too many Americans receive too many benefits from their actual or potential dealings with China for policymakers to jeopardize the relationship and because other key countries are also unwilling to confront China. Abandoning the present position and adopting a less confrontational approach might be the only way to persuade China to start cooperating.

THE BIG TWO

In part, the strategy proposed here would treat old issues in new ways, recasting conflicts as opportunities for progress. The United States and China could agree to construct their regional trade agreements in ways that support, rather than impede, subsequent multilateral liberalization—and even permit eventual linkage between the regional bodies. Failures to offer significant new market-opening opportunities in the Doha Round would be addressed not as legitimate mercantilist behavior but as threats to the WTO that would jeopardize both countries' stake in an open world economy. Competitive currency misalignments would be treated as deviations from IMF norms that hurt all trading partners, especially poor countries. Washington would concede that its errant fiscal policy has contributed to the overvaluation of the dollar, just as Beijing would concede that undervaluation of the yuan has reflected inadequate Chinese internal demand and excessive government intervention. The United States could escort China into the International Energy Agency to help organize the response of consuming countries to high oil prices.

More far-reaching steps might involve the creation of new international norms and institutional arrangements to govern issue areas that are important but currently unregulated, such as global warming and sovereign wealth funds (SWFs). To date, China has steadfastly refused to even contemplate binding constraints on its greenhouse gas emissions. So has the United States, but that stance seems likely to change dramatically after the presidential election in November, no matter who wins. An emissions regime, however, may well lead to the installation of trade barriers in participating countries against carbon-intensive products from nonparticipating countries. Moreover, global warming cannot be seriously addressed without China, which has become the world's largest polluter. Unless Washington and Beijing find ways to cooperate in attacking the problem together, the result could be a trade war between them and little or no action on the environment.

China has already indicated some skepticism about the adoption of new international guidelines, even if voluntary and nonbinding, regarding the structure and investment activities of SWFs. But the United States is championing such codes in order to permit continued foreign investment and head off the risk of protectionist domestic reactions. Since the U.S. economy is especially dependent on Chinese capital, without some new agreement a frontal clash could develop over this issue, triggered either by China's rejection of proposed new guidelines or by the United States' rejection of Chinese investments in particularly sensitive areas.

Whether in dealing with old or new issues, the basic idea would be to develop a G-2 between the United States and China to steer the global governance process. Other major powers, such as the EU and, on some issues, Japan, would of course need to be deeply involved as well. The new rules, codes, or norms could frequently be implemented through existing multilateral institutions, such as the IMF and the WTO. Some of them might work better through new worldwide organizations created to deal with truly new issues, such as a global environmental organization to manage climate-change policy. But effective systemic defenses against international economic challenges in today's world must start with active cooperation between its two dominant economies, the United States and China.

Given other powers' sensitivities, of course, it would be impolitic for Washington and Beijing to use the term "G-2" publicly. But for the strategy to work, the United States would have to give true priority to China as its main partner in managing the world economy, to some extent displacing Europe. Nothing less is likely to attract China or engage the United States sufficiently to create the effective leadership that the world so desperately needs.

Some initial steps have already been taken in this direction. After I floated the idea of a G-2 in late 2004, Robert Zoellick, in his new capacity as deputy secretary of state, which he undertook in February 2005, launched initial discussions with Chinese counterparts. In 2007, Treasury Secretary Henry Paulson escalated the engagement to what is now known as the U.S.-China Strategic Economic Dialogue, which involves the leaders of ten or so cabinet agencies in each country. The beginnings of an institutional framework for a working G-2 have thus already been put in place, and patterns of cooperation are already developing on topics such as the environment and international finance. But it is not nearly enough for China to be seen as a "responsible stakeholder." It must be seen, and accorded full rights, as a true leadership partner.

Such a relationship between a rich developed country and a poor developing one would be unprecedented in human history—as is there being a poor economic superpower, which is what China is. There are enough examples of similar cooperation on specific issues, however, to suggest that converting U.S.-Chinese disputes into systemic management issues can be extremely effective. In the late 1970s, for example, the United States was applying countervailing duties to scores of Brazilian products because Brazil's export subsidies accounted for almost half the value of all of its foreign sales. A frontal assault on the subsidies was politically unacceptable in Brazil, but the two countries agreed to cooperate closely in negotiating a new subsidy code for the General Agreement on Tariffs and Trade (the precursor to the WTO): this agreement turned out to be simultaneously the linchpin of a successful Tokyo Round of trade talks, a basis for adding an injury clause to the U.S. countervailing-duty law, and a foundation for phasing out the Brazilian subsidy policy.

Are the United States and China ready for such a substantial reorientation? Washington would need to accept China as a true partner in managing global economic affairs, the development of an intimate working relationship with an Asian country rather than its traditional European allies, and constructive collaboration with an authoritarian political regime rather than a democracy. All these changes would pose substantial challenges for U.S. policymakers and would likely encounter domestic political resistance.

China is rapidly approaching a moment when its chosen strategy of integration into the world economy will force it to assume increased responsibility for the successful functioning of that economy. China's own interests, in other words, should lead it to accept an invitation from the United States to help steer the system in a mutually acceptable direction. The Chinese today are hotly debating whether their country should proceed unilaterally or work within the international system, and an offer of true partnership could tilt the outcome of that debate decisively and constructively, raising the possibility that China could continue its upward trajectory without provoking the clashes that previous rising powers have.

If China is reluctant to get too close to the United States—say, because of continuing controversies over security issues—alternative institutional arrangements are of course available. The EU could be a member from the outset of a G-3, a group of the current global economic superpowers. The new G-5, recently created by the IMF to conduct its intensified multilateral consultative process, which adds Japan and Saudi Arabia (to represent the oil producers) into the mix, is another possibility. The central need is to embrace China in the context of a new and effective leadership grouping in light of its critical role in the world economy and its legitimate desire to be engaged in systemic management at all relevant stages of the process.

Under seven successive presidents, the United States has chosen to engage, rather than confront, China, taking the eminently sensible view that provoking an unnecessary confrontation would be profoundly contrary to U.S. interests. Given the signs that China's economic advance will continue, the same logic suggests that Washington should make every effort to engage Beijing as a true partner in steering global economic affairs. At a minimum, creating a G-2 would limit the risk of bilateral disputes escalating and disrupting the U.S.-Chinese relationship and the broader global economy. At a maximum, it could start a process that might, over time, generate sufficient trust and mutual understanding to produce active cooperation on crucial issues.

Right now, the prospects of such active cooperation are uncertain. But in addition to their differences, the two countries share many common interests, and their global economic positions are converging rather than diverging. Developing a partnership of the sort outlined here will not be easy and will take much time and effort. But the issues at stake are so important that even partial success would be worthwhile, and the only way to gauge the idea's feasibility is to try it. The upcoming negotiations to create a global strategy to counter global warming offer a compelling opportunity for just such an experiment.

A Strategic Economic Engagement

Strengthening U.S.-Chinese Ties

Henry M. Paulson, Jr.

SEPTEMBER/OCTOBER 2008

One of the first challenges the next U.S. president will face will be how to respond to China's emergence as a global power. Some people suggest that China is a threat that must be countered or contained. Others argue that its growth is an opportunity for the U.S. economy and that Washington should manage this rising power through engagement. I believe that engagement is the only path to success.

President George W. Bush chose this approach, and it has been successful. U.S.-Chinese relations are more productive today than ever before, partly because President Bush engaged Beijing and did so based on the recognition of China's twin priorities: territorial integrity and economic growth. Even if it were possible to block China's growth, it would not be in the United States' interest to try. China's rapid emergence as a global economic power presents numerous challenges on issues ranging from trade and investment to commodity markets and the environment. But the inextricable interdependence of China's growth and that of the global economy requires a policy

HENRY M. PAULSON, JR. is U.S. Secretary of the Treasury.

of engagement. In fact, the overriding importance of economic growth to China's leaders presents the best means of influencing China's emergence as a global power and encouraging its integration into the international system.

To be effective, however, Washington must first understand Beijing's interests and the challenges it faces. The Chinese see economic growth as essential to their stability. Three decades of economic development have transformed their country, bringing it peace and stability and lifting hundreds of millions of people out of poverty. The Chinese are deeply proud of these accomplishments yet are concerned about their ability to sustain them. Their leaders, meanwhile, realize that China's future growth depends on its increasing integration into global trade, investment, and financial markets.

The United States and China share many interests, but as is inevitable in any broad and complex relationship, they also have significant differences. When it comes to China's military modernization, its enforcement of intellectual property rights, and its human rights record, Washington and Beijing have strongly diverging views and sometimes competing interests. On such issues, Washington must be both direct and vigilant in its efforts to advance U.S. interests bilaterally or, where appropriate, multilaterally. Such an approach will invariably create tensions, as it sometimes does in the United States' relations with other countries. But differences with China must not be allowed to stand in the way of progress and cooperation.

The United States and China—and, indeed, the international community—share a powerful interest in China's successful integration into the global economic system. The prosperity of both nations depends on the ability of each to achieve balanced economic growth, on stable and vibrant trade and financial regimes, on diverse and dependable energy sources, and on sustainable progress that protects human health and the environment.

UNDERSTANDING CHINA

In 2006, President Bush and Chinese President Hu Jintao launched the U.S.-China Strategic Economic Dialogue (SED) to manage both immediate tensions between the two countries and their expanding relationship over the long term. The approach has worked, largely because it has recognized China's realities—seeing the country as it actually is, not as many Americans imagine it to be. Washington understands, for example, that robust and sustained economic growth is a social imperative for China and that Beijing views its international interactions primarily through an economic lens. Hence, approaching Beijing through economic issues of interest to both countries is an effective way to produce tangible results in economic and noneconomic areas.

Perhaps as a consequence of their troubled memories of the central planning, autarky, and mass mobilization of a few decades ago, China's leaders today are committed to reform, at least so long as it improves the country's political and economic stability. Every Chinese official older than the age of 50 experienced the calamities of the Great Leap Forward and the Cultural Revolution. In a country now so dynamic that entire blocks can be demolished and rebuilt in two weeks, people are searching for stability and balance. President Hu has said that it is the Chinese government's job to ensure "harmony," and this belief has reinforced Beijing's tendency toward caution in decision-making. Thus, with every policy, Beijing considers whether it is riskier to move too quickly or too slowly down the path of reform. The challenge for Washington is to understand China's perception of its self-interest, identify opportunities to persuade China that its interests and those of the United States often are the same, and narrow real differences whenever possible.

Despite the two countries' long history of interaction, they frequently display a stunning ability to misunderstand each other. A productive relationship requires that U.S. and Chinese policymakers engage at the highest levels in ways that lessen misperceptions and miscommunications. The SED accomplishes this by focusing on dialogues between top-level officials who treat one another as equals and engage on issues at the strategic level. For example, a bilateral air-services agreement was concluded during the second SED meeting, in May 2007. Lower-level negotiations on such an agreement had been stalled for some time because China was focused on developing the competitiveness of its domestic aviation industry and limiting international competition. But through the SED, I brought this issue to the attention of my counterpart, then Vice Premier Wu Yi, and explained how the increased exchange of people and goods between our two countries would strengthen their relationship. Thanks to the agreement, U.S. passenger flights to and from China will more than double by 2012, and air-cargo companies from both countries will enjoy full liberalization of the industry, including the lifting of restrictions on the frequency and price of flights, by 2011.

EQUALITY AND TRUST

The Chinese are proud of their country's emergence on the world stage and rightly seek credit for its accomplishments. After nearly two centuries of exploitation by foreign powers, China feels it is important to defend its national interests, particularly against foreign demands. Unfortunately, the United States has often been perceived as arrogant and aggressive in its interactions with China, even when it has pursued legitimate interests.

U.S. officials are more effective when they understand the Chinese people's perspective. This is one reason why I travel to China so often; nothing can substitute for personal interactions with top decision-makers, especially in China, where respect and friendship are particularly prized. My counterparts in the SED, Vice Premier Wang Qishan and, before him, then Vice Premier Wu, have emphasized the importance of mutual trust. Establishing relationships at the top of the Chinese government has been key to the U.S. government's success with the SED.

One of the reasons relationship building is so important is that government decisions in China are often made by consensus and after much consultation. Reform progresses best when an umbrella of support at the top facilitates change at lower levels. Officially, the most important decisions are made by President Hu and Premier Wen Jiabao, but unofficially, decisions are increasingly made through a consensus-oriented process involving powerful government ministries. The SED's high-level, cross-agency approach recognizes this reality and brings key decision-makers to the table to build broad support for reform.

When the SED was first launched, in September 2006, few believed much progress would be possible. I was warned, by people in the United States and China, that the timing could not be worse to discuss economic issues. The 2006 U.S. midterm elections were just months away, the U.S. presidential campaign was already taking shape, and Beijing was preparing to appoint a new generation of leaders. Nevertheless, I believed direct engagement was the only way forward: there were too many critical issues between the United States and China that simply could not be allowed to drift without strategic direction.

The result was the SED, which is led at the vice-premier level in China and by the lead economic cabinet secretary on the U.S. side, and there is cabinet-level representation from all ministries with responsibilities for economic issues. To break down traditional government silos, Chinese ministers and U.S. cabinet secretaries participate in every session, all of which my Chinese counterpart and I lead. Discussions cover a variety of strategic issues, of both immediate and long-term concern, and are mostly unstructured. Unlike in other U.S.-Chinese economic dialogues, in the SED each side's commitments are recorded and publicized at the end of the sessions and then meticulously followed up on at the highest levels to ensure that they are fully implemented.

Recognizing that the active support and engagement of the president's office on broader economic questions is very important in both countries, twice a year the U.S. and Chinese governments hold cabinet-level meetings, which include the president of the host country. I have had regular and welcome access to President Hu and Premier Wen to talk about the most important economic issues in the U.S.-Chinese relationship. In August 2007, I discussed the adverse impact of economic nationalism in both the United States and China with President Hu. I believe that our candid discussion, which focused on areas of mutual interest, such as keeping each country's market open to the other's trade and investment, gave President Hu a better understanding of why China's growth and stability depend on its moving forward with liberalization, despite resistance from its domestic industry.

The SED's interagency approach also allows all the ministers and cabinet officials to hear arguments from all sides, and that, in turn, informs the decision-making process. For example, the governor of the People's Bank of China, Zhou Xiaochuan, does not decide the pace of the renminbi's appreciation on his own; through the SED, all the ministers involved in that decision can discuss it with the U.S. representatives. During the second SED meeting, in Washington in May 2007, the chair of the Federal Reserve, Ben Bernanke, highlighted to 15 Chinese ministers the urgency of rebalancing China's growth and reforming its exchange-rate policy. Seldom in the history of U.S.-Chinese relations has there been such an opportunity to speak directly to the entire Chinese economic leadership at once on such a pressing economic challenge. Likewise, the

U.S. cabinet's understanding of China improves when it hears firsthand top Chinese policymakers explain the rationales for their positions.

Encouraging communication across stovepiped bureaucracies maximizes results. Before the SED's December 2007 meeting, China's State Environmental Protection Agency, or SEPA (since upgraded to the Ministry of Environmental Protection), had been working with the U.S. Environmental Protection Agency for years on an emissions-trading program for sulfur dioxide in China. It had conducted pilot projects at the local level but had been unsuccessful in expanding the effort nationally. After the SED brought the discussion to key offices of China's State Council, relevant Chinese ministries, and opinion leaders and companies in China, it helped SEPA gain broad support among the senior Chinese leadership, paving the way for Beijing to announce at the third SED meeting, in December 2007, that it would develop a nationwide program on sulfur-dioxide-emissions trading in the power sector. This was a meaningful step toward using market forces to address pollution and provide cleaner air in China. The move will also expand U.S. export markets and create jobs for U.S. environmental companies, which lead the world in developing the kinds of technologies necessary for such a program.

OVERLAPPING INTERESTS

By focusing on policy areas in which China's reform agenda intersects with U.S. interests, the SED has found new and constructive ways to discuss some of the most important and contentious matters in the U.S.-Chinese economic relationship, including growth imbalances, energy security and environmental sustainability, trade and investment issues (including product safety), and China's position in the global economic system. Addressing these questions not only serves the interests of the Chinese people but also is vital to both the economic strength of the United States (which welcomes access to this important export market) and the continued strength of the global economy. Americans who worry that China might overtake the United States are worrying about the wrong thing. They should instead be concerned that Beijing may not make key reforms or that it will face significant economic difficulties down the road. Serious troubles in China's economy could threaten the stability of the U.S. and global economies.

Despite the emergence of China as a global economic power—it now has the fourth-largest GDP in the world—it is still a developing country, ranking only one-hundredth in the world in per capita GDP. China's income growth has been widespread but uneven; consequently, income inequality has risen sharply in the last three decades. One indicator of this inequality is enrollment rates in China's provincial high schools, for which parents must pay fees. Earlier in the reform era, there were only small differences in such rates across provinces, but by 2003 enrollment was nearing 100 percent in the wealthier provinces, compared with less than 40 percent in the poorer ones. With China's social stability anchored in the belief that the wealth boom will eventually filter down to everyone, continued growth remains Chinese leaders' most important priority. But the challenges of sustaining growth and reducing income inequality are becoming more formidable as China's economy grows more complex, its exports begin to saturate overseas markets, its population ages, and domestic demands for a clean environment intensify.

Ironically, it is precisely the growth model that spurred China's recent takeoff that may become an obstacle to the country's sustained economic growth and social stability in the future. Over the last four decades, all emerging markets in East Asia have seen their industrial sectors grow, and many have also experienced increases in income inequality. But these shifts have been much greater in China. The country's heavy reliance on exports and investments in its capital-intensive manufacturing industry in order to support growth has promoted the rapid rise of energy consumption (as well as environmental damage), the building up of coastal areas far faster than the country's interior (where 740 million people, or more than half of the population, live), and a dramatic increase in China's trade surplus (which has heightened tensions with its trading partners).

One of the most notable indications of China's imbalanced growth is its large current account surplus, which last year amounted to over 11 percent of the country's GDP. This reflects the fact that China spends much less than it produces and earns and that it has a high rate of national saving. Chinese household consumption was only 35 percent of GDP in 2007, down from roughly 50 percent 30 years ago, when Beijing started market reforms. (Household consumption is roughly 70 percent of GDP in the United States and 60 percent in India.) On the other hand, household savings are high, as individual Chinese try to compensate for the country's thin social safety net, limited options to finance major expenditures such as education, and few investment options other than bank deposits. Demographics will only exacerbate these trends: as China's population ages, the traditional source of support in retirement—children—will become increasingly scarce.

China must further develop its financial sector to help reduce this excessive personal savings rate and boost personal consumption. With more financial products and services available to fund major expenditures and insure against misfortune, and with investment options yielding higher returns, Chinese households will be in a position to save less and consume more. A more dynamic and competitive financial sector would also channel resources for investment into the new, less capital-intensive industries, such as the services and information industries, that will drive China's growth in the future.

In order to ensure stable, noninflationary growth in the short term and sustainable growth in the long term, China also needs flexible prices and, in particular, a flexible exchange rate. Beijing's tight management of the renminbi, coupled with its large trade surplus and large capital inflows, has led to a staggering accumulation of foreign exchange reserves—now totaling over $1.8 trillion. This has prompted the People's Bank of China to issue massive amounts of renminbi so that it can buy up the foreign exchange reserves and keep the currency from appreciating too rapidly—and that, in turn, has helped fuel inflation despite the central bank's efforts to absorb the excess money by selling bonds and raising bank reserve requirements. Currency appreciation and greater flexibility in China's exchange rate could limit the impact of rising world oil and commodity prices on prices in China and at the same time allow Chinese monetary policy to be a more effective tool for ensuring stable growth. A stronger renminbi would also encourage economic activity in the sectors of the Chinese economy—particularly services—that produce for the domestic market. And this would help raise the share of household consumption in China's economy, increasing the role of domestic demand in powering China's growth and making that growth more sustainable in the future.

These issues have been at the center of many SED discussions. As a result of such talks, China's leaders have come to recognize the value of exchange-rate adjustment, in particular, and have significantly accelerated the pace of the renminbi's appreciation. Between July 2005, when the Chinese government first unpegged the renminbi from the U.S. dollar, and mid-June 2008, Beijing allowed the renminbi to appreciate against the dollar by 20 percent on a nominal basis and 23 percent on a real basis. Seventy percent of that appreciation has occurred since the SED began, and half of it over the past year alone. China clearly has much further to go, but the progress to date is an example of how strategic dialogue can yield results.

Thanks to the SED, Washington has worked steadily to help Beijing open China's financial sector, creating new opportunities for Chinese institutions to invest abroad and for U.S. banking, securities, and insurance companies to operate in China, including by enabling them to invest in China's stock markets. U.S. and other foreign financial institutions are industry leaders in China, but they face domestic competitors pushing for protection. The SED continues to explore paths by which the Chinese government can further liberalize China's financial sector, including allowing foreign companies to issue renminbi-denominated stocks and bonds and expanding the permitted scope of business for foreign securities firms.

POWERFUL CHALLENGES

As the two largest consumers and two of the largest importers of oil in the world, the United States and China are natural allies when it comes to energy security. The United States has adopted pro-market policies, pushed for transparency in energy supply and demand, and promoted the development of alternative energy sources, and it has encouraged China to do the same. Yet the United States is still urgently in need of a comprehensive energy policy to ensure its energy security. And so is China. In fact, if China today were as efficient as the United States was in 1970, it would save the equivalent of 16 million barrels of oil a day, or almost 20 percent of the world's daily oil consumption.

There are signs of change. After years of viewing energy as merely an input for economic growth, the Chinese government now increasingly recognizes the need to proactively manage its energy demand. Three key factors have motivated this transition. The first is economic. China has typically set price caps on electricity and subsidized oil in an attempt to promote social stability, but such artificially low prices have encouraged inefficient and wasteful consumption, even as the cost of these programs to the government has increased with rising global energy prices. As a result, the country now faces continued gasoline and diesel shortages, and in times of crisis, the government can no longer ensure a steady supply of energy to its people—as happened during the snowstorms of early 2008.

Second, China's leaders have recognized that resource scarcity constrains their ability to maintain political stability by improving the population's quality of life. They now realize the need to develop a new, low-energy model of economic growth. There simply are not enough energy resources to allow the world's entire population, or even the third of it represented by the Chinese, to lead the resource-intensive lifestyle that Americans currently enjoy. A way to support higher incomes while placing less of a burden on resources must be found.

The third reason Beijing is increasingly aware of the need to control energy demand is growing popular concern, especially among the middle and upper-middle classes in China, over the environmental degradation caused by inefficient energy use. Approximately 1,000 disputes over environmental protection occur each week in China. Environmental damage there is so severe that according to World Bank estimates, the combined health and nonhealth costs of air and water pollution in China amount to $100 billion a year, or about 5.8 percent of the country's GDP.

Despite the international concern linking China's energy and environmental challenges to climate change, this is not yet a pressure point for Beijing. China's leaders are acutely aware of the enormity of the problem and of its costs to China, be they floods and other natural disasters or the threat of rising sea levels to the country's coastal cities. But they face more pressing short-term, localized environmental issues—such as polluted water and air, which compromise their people's health—and they view climate change as a problem created by industrialized countries and hence one for those countries to solve. Beijing still views international discussions and negotiations on the topic as opportunities to get other countries to pay it to reduce the environmental impact of China's economic growth. Existing agreements have given Beijing reason to hope for success with this strategy: in 2007, China received 73 percent of the carbon credits available under the Clean Development Mechanism, a feature of the Kyoto Protocol that allows industrialized states to meet their obligations under the treaty by funding emissions-reduction projects in developing countries.

As China becomes the world's largest and fastest-growing emitter of carbon, the rest of the international community is recognizing that it cannot meet its goals on climate change without a major undertaking by Beijing. Fortunately, there is a constructive path forward. As China makes progress on its immediate energy and environmental challenges by making its economy less energy-intensive through the implementation of low-carbon policies, strategies, and technologies, a corollary benefit will be a reduction in the growth rate of its carbon emissions. And given China's growing role in the global economy, it will soon become clear, first to the rest of the world and then to Beijing, that the Chinese government must assume more responsibility for meeting the challenge of climate change.

Meanwhile, even as the United States and other countries grapple with multilateral treaty negotiations on climate change, the SED has focused its bilateral discussions on the costs of climate change to the United States and China. The ramifications of China's energy policies have been a consistent topic of discussion at the SED, and I have encouraged the Chinese government to move toward a market-determined price for energy. Beijing has had a plan for introducing additional market prices in the energy sector for some time but has been concerned about the instability that such a measure could cause. Beijing's decision to raise fuel prices and eliminate subsidies last June, immediately after the SED's fourth meeting and during a visit by Vice Premier Wang to Washington, was the right move: it is critical for China's stability that such reforms be made while China's economy is strong.

The United States and China recognize that both energy security and environmental protection are crucial for their sustainable development. Although the two countries have different needs and face different challenges, they both want to achieve energy security while maintaining a healthy environment. Out of this shared recognition has come one of the SED's major achievements: the signing of the Ten Year Energy and Environment Cooperation Framework at the SED last June. This framework is a bilateral mechanism focused on creating a new energy-efficient model for sustainable economic development and on addressing the factors that cause climate change through concrete actions. Recognizing that such problems are too big for either government to fix alone, the initiative involves all levels of government, business, and other sectors of society in both countries and focuses on the development and implementation of new technology, the review of current policies, the development of new regulatory and enforcement capacities, and public education. The framework has produced tangible results in the areas of electricity production and transmission, water and air quality, transportation, and forest and wetland conservation—suggesting the promise that future cooperation between the United States and China holds. Through the framework, the United States and China are already cooperating on joint research on alternative and renewable fuels for transportation and on efforts to improve the water quality of China's rivers, lakes, and streams. Even greater breakthroughs could lie in the years ahead, and this framework provides the next U.S. administration with a critically important foundation on which to continue Washington's economic engagement with China.

TRADE AND INVESTMENT

Trade and investment, once the glue of U.S.-Chinese relations, today represent a source of tension. China's recent economic reform placed the country on a clear path toward becoming a modern economy, and although it has not veered off that path, it no longer clearly embraces the elements necessary to complete its transformation. Exploiting popular anxieties about globalization, economic nationalists in China are questioning the benefits of China's integration into the international economic system.

Beijing has recently adopted policies that seek to restrict foreign access to China's markets, including a new antimonopoly law. Although much will ultimately depend on how this law is implemented, it appears to favor some of the large companies that lead domestic industries, which the Chinese government promotes as "national champions." China's foreign-investment regulations are opaque and increasingly restrictive, and the government continues to grant major subsidies to key domestic industrial sectors. Heavy lobbying by local authorities and by profitable and powerful Chinese businesses is shaping Beijing's industrial policy. As a result, both large U.S. corporations (longtime proponents of bilateral engagement) and smaller U.S. businesses (which are eager to enter new markets in China) are growing concerned about the lack of openness to U.S. products in China. And those U.S. companies with major investments in China have no consistent way to protect them.

Thus, the launching of negotiations for a bilateral investment treaty during the June 2008 SED meeting was particularly important for both countries, as such a treaty would protect the large amount of U.S. investment in China and open up new opportunities for U.S. investors while encouraging more Chinese investment in the United States. The initiative was also significant because China, as the greatest beneficiary of the market reforms it has undertaken, has the most to lose from slowing down or reversing these reforms, and the initiative would keep it on the reform track. As the United States itself has learned, promoting competition and innovation, especially through the protection of intellectual property rights and the advancement of transparency and the rule of law, is essential to sustaining robust economic growth in the long term.

There are serious obstacles ahead, however. Economic nationalism, for one thing, has been a growing concern in the United States in recent years. Low-cost imports, particularly from China, sometimes have a negative image among the American public, even though they have helped the United States contain inflation and both maximized the choice of products available to Americans and minimized their costs. Foreign investment into the United States, especially by sovereign wealth funds and state-owned enterprises, is also increasingly viewed with suspicion by some U.S. companies, various members of the national security community, and the American public at large, despite regulations by the Committee on Foreign Investment in the United States that provide sufficient protections in sensitive sectors.

These concerns are misplaced. Like many countries accumulating large foreign exchange reserves, China is simply looking for profitable places to invest them over the long term. China invests its reserves in U.S. securities, including U.S. Treasuries, but there is little Chinese direct investment in the United States. This is largely because Chinese companies are just beginning to invest in their export markets and are unsure whether they are welcome. In any event, the United States would do well to encourage such investment from anywhere in the world— including China—because it represents a vote of confidence in the U.S. economy and it promotes growth, jobs, and productivity in the United States.

The size of the bilateral trade imbalance—$256.2 billion in 2007—has also been a bone of contention. It is a source of anxiety in both the United States and China. Beijing believes that the trade deficit could be reduced if Washington dropped export controls and allowed sensitive technologies that may also have military applications to reach Chinese markets. In fact, U.S. export controls have only a marginal effect on the bilateral trade imbalance: in 2007, export license applications were required for $9.7 billion worth of U.S. goods destined for China, and just 0.7 percent of these applications were denied—a drop in the bucket. Removing all export controls in 2007 would have affected only 0.0265 percent of the U.S.-Chinese trade deficit.

A real issue is the inadequate protection of intellectual property rights in China, which has been an obstacle to increased U.S. trade with and investment in China and has prevented a reduction in the bilateral trade imbalance. This and the theft or pirating of goods are big problems for many U.S. companies operating in China and a reason others are reluctant to do business there. To protect themselves, some U.S. companies purposefully introduce older products into the Chinese market, releasing the newer goods only once the older ones have been copied.

But these and other strategies are merely stopgap measures. As China pursues its quest to develop a modern economy focused on technology, the Chinese government and Chinese companies will increasingly recognize the need to reward the creativity of their own firms and entrepreneurs by strengthening and enforcing intellectual property laws and regulations. It is by improving and enforcing its intellectual property laws that China will accelerate the development and competitiveness of its economy and also open up new market opportunities in China for companies around the world.

CHINA AND THE GLOBAL ECONOMY

China's return to the world stage as a global economic power has greater consequences than the rise of other nations with comparable per capita incomes. This is partly because few economies at China's level of development have had to address such a complex array of regulatory and governance challenges. Major developed economies are demanding that China do more than most developing nations at an equivalent stage of development. Given its substantial impact on the global economy, China must accept greater responsibilities. If it does not, other countries are likely to blame it for many of their own economic problems. China is already cited as an example of the ills of globalization, such as unsafe products and job losses in other countries. It risks further endangering its reputation, which could hurt its economic growth in the long term. As a country deeply invested in the global economic system, China would benefit from playing an increasingly proactive role in global economic decision-making. And yet it seems to be doing the opposite in the Doha Round of international trade negotiations. Its insistence on protecting its own industrial development is driving other countries to do the same and has been a major factor in the growing antiglobalization and protectionist sentiment around the world.

This point notwithstanding, China's diplomacy has been more effective than is often acknowledged. China has been deft in exercising its soft power to advance its economic interests around the world. In 2006, it hosted the first summit and third ministerial conference of the Forum on China-Africa Cooperation, inviting delegations from nearly 50 countries in Africa to Beijing for a weeklong celebration of China's growing relationship with the continent. At the conference's conclusion, Beijing pledged to unconditionally double its aid to Africa by 2009—thus indirectly opening the door to additional Chinese investment in the continent. China's bilateral engagement has generally focused on developing mutually beneficial economic objectives. Some of the resulting relationships, such as those with Angola and Sudan, have occasionally been at odds with international norms or have undermined the World Bank's efforts to promote transparency. But Beijing now recognizes that its future economic growth is tied to the continued success of the global system, and it is beginning to contribute more to the international community. It is becoming a more responsible trading and investment partner in Africa and Latin America, for example. In 2007, China contributed for the first time to the International Development Association, the branch of the World Bank that provides grants and low-interest credit to the world's poorest countries. It now collaborates with the World Bank on projects in Africa. It has recently joined the Financial Action Task Force, the multilateral organization that assesses countries' efforts to combat money laundering and terrorist financing. And it is in talks to join the Inter-American Development Bank. U.S. officials have encouraged these efforts through the SED and so facilitated China's integration into the global economic system.

Beijing has recently realized some of the unpleasant implications of working outside the global economic system, especially in the energy sector. It has tended to pursue a mercantilist policy regarding energy security in an attempt to protect itself against the price fluctuations and supply disruptions intrinsic to the global oil market. But its attempts to lock in oil supplies by investing in facilities in troubled countries such as Iran and Sudan have not succeeded. China has paid above-market prices for overseas exploration and extraction projects, and these efforts have helped it meet only five percent of its demand in imported oil; it still depends on global markets to meet the remaining 95 percent. China is simply too large a nation with too great a domestic demand to buy its way to energy security. Moreover, as Beijing has recently begun to recognize, the cost of doing business with sketchy governments comes at a substantial political price. China's investments in Sudan, for example, have tarnished its international reputation. Concerns have emerged among the Chinese people, too, after several Chinese citizens were caught and killed by Sudanese rebels in Darfur. Likewise, as Tehran continues to face censure for its nuclear-development activities, Beijing is gradually realizing that doing business in Iran is becoming increasingly complex and increasingly costly to its image.

Like China's top officials, China's business leaders have begun to recognize the negative impact of China's reputation as an opportunist. The China National Offshore Oil Corporation, or CNOOC, has been paying more and more attention to social responsibility and is making it one of the tenets of the company's oil-exploration activities around the world. Through the SED, the U.S. government has worked to foster Beijing's awareness that China, like the United States, is a stakeholder in the global economic system. Washington has encouraged Beijing, for instance, to join the Congo Basin Forest Partnership, an initiative that promotes the sustainable management of resources in the Congo River Basin. And these efforts are making a difference. At the SED meeting last June, the two governments agreed for the first time to work together to promote global sustainable forest management. Change is occurring as Beijing recognizes the benefits of participating in and contributing to the international system.

LOOKING AHEAD

Going forward, there are three possible ways for the United States and China to pursue their economic and trade relations: robust engagement, dispute resolution through multilateral and bilateral enforcement measures, or punitive legislation. Since a retributive policy would be counterproductive and would harm U.S. economic interests, the U.S. government has chosen the first two approaches.

And rightly so. Since Washington stepped up its economic

engagement with Beijing through the SED two years ago, the U.S.-Chinese relationship has deepened and expanded. By encouraging top-level discussions of the two countries' long-term strategic priorities, the SED has found effective ways to manage short-term tensions surrounding trade disputes. It has alleviated a complex set of concerns in the U.S. Congress in a way that has led to a significant appreciation of the renminbi and forestalled dangerous protectionist legislation. At the same time that U.S. consumers were growing deeply concerned about product safety, the SED developed a comprehensive plan for improving the quality and regulatory oversight of foods and drugs imported from China (the effort could even serve as a global model for product safety). And as the world was becoming more eager to reduce its dependence on oil, the SED initiated the Ten Year Energy and Environment Cooperation Framework to help expedite the United States' and China's efforts to increase their energy efficiency. The SED has enabled progress on significant noneconomic issues and more progress on economic issues than otherwise would have occurred.

These successes have created a foundation of mutual understanding and trust and a platform for further progress. History has shown that the ties between the United States and China have been most stable and mutually beneficial when a common interest has united leaders in Washington and Beijing. During the Cold War, balancing the Soviet Union's power in Asia was that shared interest. It generated trust for a very young U.S.-Chinese relationship and facilitated substantial bilateral cooperation. Now, the SED has reoriented U.S.-Chinese relations based on the strategic rationale of sustaining global economic growth. This unifying theme will motivate policymakers in both countries and offers the chance to redefine the terms of the two countries' relationship from simple cooperation to joint management and, perhaps eventually, even genuine partnership. Such a recasting will be an invitation to China to participate in global affairs as an equal—a position that Beijing covets.

I have learned firsthand that the United States is much more effective at resolving global issues when it approaches them multilaterally rather than unilaterally. On every major economic, political, and security issue, the path that China chooses will affect the United States' ability to achieve its goals. This will also be true under the next U.S. administration. The SED must be used to help manage the myriad economic issues that will undoubtedly arise and help keep the vital U.S.-Chinese relationship on an even keel, productively advancing shared interests while working through enduring differences. It is possible to manage these challenges in a way that advances both U.S. and Chinese interests. And it is my hope that the next U.S. president will expand on the SED to take U.S.-Chinese relations to the next level.

The G-2 Mirage

Why the United States and China Are Not Ready to Upgrade Ties

Elizabeth C. Economy and Adam Segal

MAY/JUNE 2009

It took just one month for U.S. President Barack Obama's foreign policy team to establish its line on China: more cooperation on more issues more often. As Secretary of State Hillary Clinton enthusiastically declared during her brief visit to Beijing in late February, "The opportunities for us to work together are unmatched anywhere in the world."

The Obama team is in good company. Henry Kissinger has called for the U.S.-Chinese relationship to be "taken to a new level" and Zbigniew Brzezinski has advocated the development of a G-2, a group of two comprising China and the United States that could address the international financial crisis, tackle climate change, limit the proliferation of weapons of mass destruction, and maybe even help resolve the Israeli-Palestinian conflict. Early notes of potential discord—Treasury Secretary Timothy Geithner's description of China as a currency manipulator, Secretary Clinton's call for greater religious freedom in

ELIZABETH C. ECONOMY is C. V. Starr Senior Fellow and Director for Asia Studies at the Council on Foreign Relations. ADAM SEGAL is Maurice R. Greenberg Senior Fellow for China Studies at the Council on Foreign Relations.

China, National Intelligence Director Dennis Blair's openness to potential future arms sales to Taiwan—were muted in the interest of elevating the U.S.-Chinese relationship.

Calling on the United States and China to do more together has an undeniable logic. Both Washington and Beijing are destined to fail if they attempt to confront the world's problems alone, and the current bilateral relationship is not getting the job done. Real coordination on trade and currency reform remains stunted, both sides lag behind the rest of the world in addressing climate change, and meaningful partnership on global challenges—from food safety to nuclear proliferation—is limited.

But elevating the bilateral relationship is not the solution. It will raise expectations for a level of partnership that cannot be met and exacerbate the very real differences that still exist between Washington and Beijing. The current lack of U.S.-Chinese cooperation does not stem from a failure on Washington's part to recognize how much China matters, nor is it the result of leaders ignoring the bilateral relationship. It derives from mismatched interests, values, and capabilities.

The United States must accordingly resist the temptation to initiate a high-profile, high-stakes bilateral dialogue and instead embrace a far more flexible, multilateral approach to China. In other words, Obama should continue to work with China in order to address global problems, but he also needs to enlist the world to deal with the problems created by the rise of China.

The good news is that the United States and China do share some fundamental foreign policy goals: kickstarting economic growth and maintaining an open global economy, maintaining peace and stability in East Asia, and halting climate change. There is already a robust process of government-to-government exchange, with more than 60 bilateral dialogues and working groups in existence, including the Strategic Economic Dialogue, the U.S.-China Senior Dialogue, and the Defense

Policy Coordination Talks. The United States and China have cooperated on counterterrorism, negotiated with North Korea through the six-party talks, and undertaken joint research on alternative energy. Recently, the Pentagon welcomed the deployment of the Chinese navy for antipiracy operations in the Gulf of Aden, where both the United States and China depend on the same shipping lanes.

Recognition of China's importance, however, cannot paper over the difficulties the two countries have faced—and will continue to face—as they try to convert shared strategic goals into concrete cooperation. Even after 30 years of engagement, the United States and China still disagree about how the world should work. When there is agreement on the principles of global governance, more narrow economic interests or differences in political values typically make a common front elusive. And even when shared values and interests allow the two sides to move forward, the vast gap in governance and implementation capabilities often leads to mutual frustration and recriminations.

THE GREAT STALL

A significant obstacle to effective U.S.-Chinese cooperation is the dramatically different view of sovereignty, sanctions, and the use of force that each country brings to the table. Beijing's need for resources and export markets, along with its oft-repeated mantra of not mixing business with politics, clashes with the West's efforts to prevent human rights abuses and improve governance in the developing world. For example, Chinese state-owned companies have vast resource holdings and development interests in countries such as Angola, the Democratic Republic of the Congo, and Myanmar (also called Burma), where human rights abuses and problems of poor governance are rampant. Likewise, China's refusal to stop its growing arms trade has contributed to instability in Sudan and Zimbabwe, even as the rest of the world has urged restraint in weapons sales to those nations. Yet Beijing repeatedly refuses to exert its economic leverage for political ends, arguing that the political and economic realms should remain separate.

Although Washington and Beijing share some common interests in Darfur, Myanmar, and other regions in which serious human rights violations are occurring, their opposing perspectives on sovereignty and humanitarian intervention lead to very different policy prescriptions. In September 2007, for example, Beijing, along with Moscow, blocked a UN Security Council resolution sponsored by the United States and Europe that forcefully condemned the Myanmar government for the use of force against Buddhist monks who were leading antigovernment protests. China, which has strong political ties to Myanmar's rulers and large investments in oil and gas projects in the country, insisted that the crackdown was an internal affair, called for restraint, and finally voted for a much-watered-down resolution.

Beijing's growing dependence on imported oil and gas has also been an obstacle to broader U.S.-Chinese cooperation on limiting Iran's nuclear program. China has generally rejected calls for tough sanctions against Iran and undermined efforts by the United States and Europe to stop the flow of Iranian money through foreign banks. As Iran's trade with the European Union (EU) has declined, it has picked up with China.

In addition, China's authoritarian but decentralized political and economic system also makes cooperation on issues such as product safety and environmental protection difficult. Beijing is often incapable of following through on its international obligations because local actors have strong economic incentives to maintain the status quo. Even when the central government has the best intentions, a lack of transparency and accountability further undermines the implementation of laws. Over the past several years, for example, China's food- and product-safety records have come under increasing international scrutiny. China's vast exports ensure that almost no country goes unaffected when tainted pet food, toothpaste, dairy products, toys, or pharmaceutical ingredients are released onto the market. These poisonous products have entered the EU, Japan, Panama, the United States, and Vietnam—to name just a few. Efforts to address China's ongoing problems in the realm of food and product safety are hampered not only by bureaucracies with weak oversight capacity but also by a government that refuses to permit the media and on-the-ground watchdogs to investigate and warn the general public. Reporters from *Southern Weekend* and the *Oriental Morning Post* knew two months before the story became public, in September 2008, that melamine—a chemical that suppliers were adding to low-quality dairy products in order raise the protein level and pass inspections—had sickened children. But they were prohibited from reporting the news, in order to ensure a positive atmosphere for the Olympics. Although the press, bloggers, and nongovernmental organizations are becoming increasingly assertive, they are unable to act consistently as a check on local officials due to censorship and political harassment.

Cooperation on climate change may prove even more challenging. As Washington weighs the value of pursuing a bilateral climate deal with China, Beijing's ability to enforce regulations will be called into question. Effective climate policy depends on transparency in reporting emissions, yet in the run-up to the Olympics, Beijing's published air-pollution index did not include two of the most dangerous pollutants: ozone and small particulate matter. A bilateral climate deal would also necessitate large-scale transfers of energy-related technologies, such as advanced materials for wind turbines, from the United States to China. However, China lacks the legal infrastructure needed to enforce intellectual property rights—a weakness that will worry the European, Japanese, and U.S. firms that design new green technologies. Even basic policy initiatives, such as the implementation of energy-efficient building codes, require a degree of enforcement capacity and official accountability that does not exist within the Chinese government.

A lack of transparency has also been a consistent barrier to improving the bilateral military relationship, which has consisted of high-level discussions about strategic issues as well as lower-level exchanges and working groups. As the defense scholars Kurt Campbell and Richard Weitz have argued, secrecy makes sense from the Chinese point of view; China is the weaker power and believes that uncertainty about its true capabilities can act as a deterrent. The United States, in contrast, believes transparency on the part of China would help avoid miscalculation and mishaps. Transparency is also critical when dealing with political fallout in the event of mistakes, such as the U.S. bombing of the Chinese embassy in Belgrade in May 1999 or the collision of a U.S. spy plane and a Chinese fighter jet in April 2001. Without such transparency, the United States and China's neighbors are reduced to gauging Beijing's intentions from its capabilities—a problematic proxy. The roughly 1,000 missiles targeted at Taiwan and the submarines and advanced weapons systems China has acquired—apparently to target a U.S. aircraft carrier group—all raise questions about the seriousness of Beijing's commitment to an improved military relationship with the United States.

The economic relationship is also a contentious issue. There are serious differences between what the two countries want and when they want it. Washington insists on currency reform, more open markets, and the protection of intellectual property rights. Beijing, by contrast, generally wants to be left alone to conduct its business as it sees fit or, at the very least, to ensure that Washington does not make things worse for China in the pursuit of its own agenda. Even when China has engaged directly on economic issues—such as the protection of intellectual property rights—it has viewed its efforts, given the difficulties of building an effective legal system, in terms of change over decades, a timetable completely out of line with the United States' much greater expectations.

The global economic crisis may well diminish these traditional differences between the trading partners. It has brought into sharp relief the extraordinary level of global economic interdependence, particularly between the United States and China. A stable recovery of the U.S. economy will require continued support from China, and China's future growth will also depend on the involvement of the United States and other nations. The relationship is no longer a matter of Washington banging on Beijing's door, alternately cajoling and hectoring Chinese leaders to reform their country's economy. Rather, the Chinese leadership, greatly concerned about the security of China's investment in U.S. Treasury bonds, the value of the dollar, and the loss of China's critical U.S. export markets, is calling on Washington to quickly respond to the global financial crisis as well as suggesting that it might expect some sort of quid pro quo—the lifting of U.S. restrictions on some technology sales, for example—for the continued purchase of U.S. Treasuries. Like their Washington counterparts, however, China's leaders will find that achieving real leverage in the context of a bilateral relationship is elusive.

THE COSTS OF COOPERATION

Although the United States needs to coordinate with China to respond to global challenges, elevating the bilateral relationship is more likely to lead to a quagmire, with recriminations flying back and forth, than to a successful partnership. To escape this downward spiral, Washington must solicit the help of the rest of the world. The United States is not alone in recognizing that China affects all the critical issues of the day or in seeking more from China as an emerging global power. Throughout the world, countries are realizing that the issues that currently define their relationships with Beijing cannot simply be negotiated bilaterally.

As a first step, the Obama administration should sit down with Japan, the EU, and other key allies to begin coordinating their policies toward China. Much of what the United States does, or is proposing to do, with China on the environment, human rights, and food and product safety is also being discussed or undertaken by Canada, the EU, Japan, and other states in Asia. Yet there is presently no coordination, which means these simultaneous efforts will be inefficient and may work at cross-purposes.

Despite insistent calls for a bilateral U.S.-Chinese effort to address climate change, cooperation would be managed best by involving other nations. The United States and China are the two largest emitters of carbon dioxide, and each is using the other as an excuse for inaction. China is currently calling for all the advanced industrialized nations to devote one percent of their GDPs to a climate fund for developing countries—a mechanism that would subsidize the transfer of clean-energy technologies to Beijing. The United States simply does not have the financial resources available to respond to this challenge. Meanwhile, Japan is pursuing a different tack and has already started to provide development assistance to China for clean-energy projects thanks to its highly sophisticated public-private partnerships that provide government financing for privately held Japanese technology companies. Beijing and Tokyo are moving ahead with technical cooperation and demonstration projects to capture and store carbon, enhance energy efficiency, and exploit renewable energy resources.

It makes sense for the United States to duplicate some of these efforts. After all, China is a large country, and there will always be unmet demand. In addition, the United States has a comparative advantage when it comes to training Chinese officials, monitoring greenhouse gas emissions, and designing some clean-energy technologies. But Washington does not want to undermine European and Japanese efforts by competing to cooperate with China. There is frequently a cost to cooperating with Beijing: Chinese government agencies often require donations or impose high overhead costs on foreign partners, and these fees could well rise as the Chinese play foreign actors off against one another. Moreover, Chinese energy and environmental agencies are woefully understaffed and often unable to meet the demands of in-depth cooperation with a number of different partners. There is also a very real danger that U.S. officials will raise expectations within China but fail to deliver if, for example, the U.S. government does not provide adequate funding for demonstration projects or training programs, as has happened with past cooperative energy and environmental ventures.

There is a similar lack of capacity for the enforcement of food- and product-safety initiatives. The U.S. Food and Drug Administration opened three offices in China with a total staff of 13 people—an admirable beginning but far from sufficient. At the same time, the EU and the Association of Southeast Asian Nations (ASEAN) are running their own food-safety programs with China, and Japan and South Korea have begun negotiations with China on the topic. A single, integrated response would be far more effective, and consumers worldwide would be much safer if U.S. inspectors worked alongside their European, Japanese, and South Korean colleagues.

As the global economic crisis deepens, trade will become an area ripe for multilateralism. For much of the last decade, while China ran up large trade surpluses with the United States and Europe, its overall trade was fairly balanced—with a total annual surplus fluctuating between one and two percent of GDP. It began rising in 2005, and by 2008 China's global trade surplus had exploded, reaching approximately 8.5 percent of

GDP. Because other countries are now suffering from similar trade imbalances with China, the United States has the opportunity to work with China's other trading partners to push China to continue to revalue its currency, reduce its export subsidies, and open its domestic market. If approached multilaterally, these demands could be framed in the context of global, rather than bilateral, imbalances.

Regional security could also benefit from greater U.S.-Chinese cooperation and from the expansion of multilateral security exchanges. China currently participates in ASEAN's security discussions and has undertaken some training and military exchanges with several of the United States' allies in Asia. A more robust cooperation effort on the part of Japan, South Korea, the United States, and other maritime countries in the region would help define the basic ground rules as China's military operates farther and farther away from the mainland. The March 2009 incident at sea, during which a U.S. Navy surveillance ship was surrounded by five Chinese vessels in the vicinity of a Chinese submarine base, suggests the need to act sooner rather than later. Moreover, additional security exchanges could help persuade Beijing that its lack of military transparency undermines regional security and—by making it more difficult for Beijing to convince its neighbors that China's rise will be peaceful—costs China politically.

Finally, Washington will need to look beyond its traditional international allies to help enhance its leverage over Beijing. China often ignores calls from the United States and Europe for political reform and a more activist foreign policy, yet it expends considerable energy positioning itself as a leader of the developing world. On sensitive political issues, if the United States worked with the same developing countries China purports to represent—African countries on Darfur, island nations on climate change, ASEAN countries on Myanmar—this might be more effective in changing China's behavior than yet another call for action from Brussels or Tokyo. On the most sensitive political issues, such as China's domestic human rights record, partnering with developing democracies could give the United States more moral suasion.

BEYOND DIALOGUE

Expanding all these partnerships will require Washington to change its behavior, too. Inconsistency between rhetoric and action undermines U.S. legitimacy, both with China and with much of the rest of the world. Many throughout the world want to see Washington live by the same rules it is pushing China to adopt. The transparency and accountability the United States demands of China and advocates within the global financial system must be implemented at home first.

Potential partners will expect the new Obama administration to fulfill its promise to shut down the U.S. prison camp at Guantánamo, overcome congressional resistance to ending some types of agricultural subsidies in the next round of Doha trade talks, and put forth a realistic and aggressive climate-change action plan that is commensurate with the United States' contribution to the problem.

Other countries will need to step up, too. The EU countries have been unable to forge a consistent policy toward China, with the member states divided over the issue of Tibet and over the wisdom of lifting the arms embargo on Beijing, which was imposed after the 1989 Tiananmen Square massacre and seems an anachronism to some. The situation looks even worse in Japan, which is suffering from an economic recession and political paralysis. Yet U.S.-Japanese cooperation on China over issues such as climate change, naval security, and product safety should resonate well with the Japanese leadership.

Engaging the rest of the world does not mean ignoring China. The United States and China should reconfigure their relationship at an institutional level. In addition to all of the existing, issue-specific exchanges, there should be one over-arching negotiation that sits above or outside the purview of the U.S. government's traditional cabinet-level agencies. The National Security Council and the vice president's office would ideally play a central role in this effort. Cooperation on the trade imbalance, a climate deal, and regional security depends on the close coordination of numerous bureaucracies within the U.S. government. Institutionally adjusting the level of the dialogue on the U.S. side would make it a bureaucratic prior-ity on the Chinese side as well, increasing the likelihood that the right Chinese officials will be at the table. Similarly, a more centralized U.S. approach to China will lead to more effective cooperation with U.S. allies.

The year 2009 marks 30 years since the normalization of relations between the United States and China. Three decades of peace and stability in U.S.-Chinese relations should be cel-ebrated. Further elevating the bilateral relationship, however, without addressing the very real differences in values and enforcement capacities between the two countries will lead nowhere—except to the creation of more empty frameworks for dialogues and never-ending dialogues to establish more frameworks. The time has come to acknowledge that although working with China sounds easy, it is not. If the United States wants to move its relationship with China forward for the next 30 years, it needs the rest of the world, not just China, on board.

Review Essay

The Unbalanced Triangle

What Chinese-Russian Relations Mean for the United States

Stephen Kotkin

SEPTEMBER/OCTOBER 2009

Axis of Convenience: Moscow, Beiing, and the New Geopolitics. By Bobo Lo. Brookings Institution Press, 2008, 277 pp. $32.95

Bobo Lo, a former Australian diplomat in Moscow and the director of the China and Russia programs at the Center for European Reform, in London, has written the best analysis yet of one of the world's more important bilateral relationships. His close examination of Chinese-Russian relations—sometimes mischaracterized by both countries as a "strategic partnership"—lays bare the full force of China's global strategy, the conundrum of Russia's place in today's world, and fundamental shortcomings in U.S. foreign policy.

China's shift in strategic orientation from the Soviet Union to the United States is the most important geopolitical

STEPHEN KOTKIN is Professor of History and International Affairs at Princeton University. His latest book is *Uncivil Society: 1989 and the Implosion of the Communist Establishment*, which includes a contribution by Jan Gross.

realignment of the last several decades. And Beijing now enjoys not only excellent relations with Washington but also better relations with Moscow than does Washington. Lo calls the Chinese-Russian relationship a "mutually beneficial partnership" and goes so far as to deem Moscow's improved ties with Beijing "the greatest Russian foreign policy achievement of the post-Soviet period."

Precisely such hyperbole drives the alarmism of many pundits, who believe that the United States faces a challenge from a Chinese-Russian alliance built on shared illiberal values. But as Lo himself argues, the twaddle about Russia being an energy superpower was dubious even before the price of oil fell by nearly $100 in 2008. Even more important, Lo points out that the Chinese-Russian relationship is imbalanced and fraught: the two countries harbor significant cultural prejudices about each other and have divergent interests that are likely to diverge even more in the future. More accurately, the Chinese-Russian relationship is, as Lo puts it, an "axis of convenience"—that is, an inherently limited partnership conditioned on its ability to advance both parties' interests.

But even Lo does not go far enough in his debunking of the Chinese-Russian alliance: he argues that it "is, for all its faults, one of the more convincing examples of positive-sum international relations today." This is doubtful. The relationship may allow the Chinese to extract strategically important natural resources from Russia and extend their regional influence, but it affords the Russians little more than the pretense of a multipolar world in which Moscow enjoys a central role.

STRATEGIC MISTRUST

The year 2006 was the Year of Russia in China, and 2007, the Year of China in Russia, with both states hosting a slew of exhibits, cultural programs, trade talks, and state visits. At the opening ceremony in Moscow in March 2007, Chinese President Hu Jintao remarked, "The Chinese National Exhibition in Russia is the largest-ever overseas display of Chinese culture and economic development." (It is worth noting that every year could be called the Year of China in the United States and that the U.S. consumer market is essentially one endless Chinese National Exhibition.)

By showcasing in Moscow 15,000 Chinese products from 30 industries—machinery, aviation, ship building, information technology, home appliances—Beijing sent the message that regardless of the substantial role the Soviet Union played in China's post-1949 industrialization, there is now a new ascendancy, with China enjoying the dominant position. This, in fact, is a return to the historical paradigm—China has generally set the agenda for relations between the two countries. The Chinese-Russian relationship dates from the Russian conquest of Siberia in the seventeenth century. The Russian empire, then not very rich, sought to trade with China, then the world's wealthiest country. The two empires also discovered a common but often rivalrous interest in crushing the Central Asian nomads, leaving China and Russia with a 2,700-mile border, the world's longest. Since then, this shared border has shifted numerous times and served as a source of intermittent tension. As recently as 1969, the two countries clashed along the Ussuri River, which separates northeastern China from the Russian Far East, and Soviet leaders discussed retaliating with nuclear weapons if China launched a mass assault.

Now, as Lo writes, their relations are, in many ways, better than ever. In June 2005, both sides ratified a treaty settling their border disputes. Cross-border business and tourism are brisk. In 2006, two million Russian tourists went to China and nearly one million Chinese visited Russia.

Still, as Lo subtly demonstrates, the Chinese-Russian "axis of convenience" is bedeviled by "pervasive mistrust" rooted in historical grievances, geopolitical competition, and structural factors. Moreover, it is a secondary axis. China and Russia talk about being strategic partners, but neither actually is central to the other's concerns. China's indispensable partner is the United States; Russia's is Europe or, more specifically, Germany. In 2007, Chinese-Russian trade reached $48 billion, up from $5.7 billion in 1999, making China Russia's second-largest trading partner after the European Union. But current Russian-EU trade exceeds $250 billion—the lion's share of it being between Russia and Germany—and Chinese-U.S. trade exceeds $400 billion. China and Russia, Lo demonstrates, "pay far more attention to the West than they do to each other." Their relationship is opportunistic. As Lo puts it, the two giants "share neither a long-term vision of the world nor a common understanding of their respective places in it."

In addition—and this is the most important aspect of Lo's argument—whatever opportunity does exist in the relationship, China is in a better position to exploit it. China extracts considerable practical benefits in oil and weapons from Russia. In return, Beijing flatters Moscow with rhetoric about their "strategic partnership" and coddles it by promoting the illusion of a multipolar world. In many ways, the Chinese-Russian relationship today resembles that which first emerged in the seventeenth century: a rivalry for influence in Central Asia alongside attempts to expand bilateral commercial ties, with China in the catbird seat. Lo politely calls this incongruity an "asymmetry."

GIVING AWAY THE STORE

The profound asymmetry in Chinese-Russian relations is most visibly illustrated by the two countries' roles in the Shanghai Cooperation Organization (SCO), a six-member security group founded in 2001, and by their energy and weapons trades.

So far, China has consistently resisted Moscow's lobbying

for building the SCO—whose other members are the former Soviet states of Kazakhstan, Kyrgyzstan, Tajikistan, and Uzbekistan—into a quasi-military alliance that could counter NATO. In addition, the SCO declined to publicly endorse Russia's account of its August 2008 war with Georgia (Moscow claimed that the Georgian army attacked first, an assertion implicitly recognized even by the U.S. ambassador to Russia). China, it seems, is unwilling to impart any strategic significance to disputes in the Caucasus.

Meanwhile, using the SCO and business investments, China has been making economic inroads into Central Asia, a region that Russia has traditionally considered within its sphere of influence. Chinese companies have been on a buying spree in recent years, making investments throughout Central Asia in minerals, energy, and other industries. Beijing appears to have cracked even the difficult nut of Turkmenistan—a pipeline now under construction is slated to run from the natural gas fields in Turkmenistan to Xinjiang, in western China. To a large extent, it is Russia's single-minded focus on pushing the United States out of Central Asia—lobbying Kyrgyzstan, for example, to eject U.S. forces from a military base in Bishkek—that has allowed China's influence there to grow relatively unhindered. And whereas the United States can scarcely hope to maintain a permanent presence in Central Asia, China can be counted on to stick around.

Lo is doubtful about the prospects of a major Chinese-Russian energy deal. But in February 2009, after his book had gone to press, the two governments signed a deal under which Rosneft, the largest Russian state-owned oil company, and Transneft, the Russian state-owned oil-pipeline monopoly, would get $25 billion from the China Development Bank in exchange for supplying China with 300,000 barrels of oil a day from 2011 to 2030—or a total of about 2.2 billion barrels. Factoring in the interest payments the Russian companies will owe on the loan, the deal means that China will pay under $20 a barrel—less than half the global price at the time of the deal and less than one-third the market price for future deliveries in 2017.

This Chinese money is slated to underwrite the completion of an oil pipeline that will run from eastern Siberia to the Pacific Ocean, with an offshoot going to Daqing to serve the Chinese market. The proposed pipeline would increase roughly to eight percent Russia's share of China's oil imports, up from four percent now. Russian energy companies, laden with debt, lack the capital to build the pipeline by themselves or, for that matter, to drill for new hydrocarbons. With a projected capacity of 600,000 barrels per day, the pipeline is expected to supply Japan with Russian oil, too—provided enough is available. Still, the $20-a-barrel price borders on the shocking. Considering the perhaps more advantageous energy deals that have been on the table with U.S. and European multinationals, Rosneft and Transeft's deal with China looks like a giveaway. It appears to be a consequence of the obsession many Russian officials have with denying the United States a strategic foothold in Russia's energy sector at all costs—even if one of those costs is opening themselves up to exploitation by the Chinese.

Energy is not even the most fruitful aspect of China's relationship with Russia. According to U.S. estimates, Russia supplies China with 95 percent of its military hardware, including Kilo-class submarines and Sovremenny-class destroyers. So far, Russian officials have not viewed the buildup of the Chinese navy as a direct threat to Russia; instead, they see it as a potential problem for Japan and the United States. Also, the post-Soviet Russian military was long unable to afford weapons produced by domestic manufacturers, making arms exports a necessity. Still, whatever benefits Russia gained by keeping its defense industry alive while waiting for better times, the benefits to China have been beyond compare. After the

Tiananmen Square crackdown in 1989, many of the world's largest arms merchants—France, the United Kingdom, and the United States—imposed an arms embargo on China. As Russia moved to fill this gap, China began to reverse engineer weapons systems and pressure Russia to sell it not just the finished products but also the underlying manufacturing technology. For reasons that have yet to be explained publicly, Russian arms sales to China have declined in recent years. Nonetheless, China has the money and remains an eager customer for Russia's blueprints.

According to Lo, the terms of Chinese-Russian trade "are becoming more unbalanced every year"—so much so that he compares the role of Russia for China to that of Angola, China's largest trading partner in Africa. Russia will remain important as long as the weapons and fossil fuels keep flowing (and no economically viable alternatives to hydrocarbons emerge). Lo does not say so explicitly, but in an imagined multipolar world, Russia looks like a Chinese subsidiary. China treats Russia with supreme tact, vehemently denying its own superiority—a studious humility that only helps it maintain the upper hand.

WHAT KIND OF PARTNER?

Lo quotes Yuri Fedorov, a Russian political analyst, who laments that Russia is "doomed to be a junior partner to everyone." In fact, it is China that has accepted the role of junior partner to the United States, and the payoff has been impressive. It is a calculated position and part of China's global strategy sometimes known as "peaceful rise," a term first introduced by the Chinese leadership soon after the Tiananmen massacre. One vital element of this strategy is for China to take advantage of its de facto strategic partnership with the United States while sometimes swallowing hard in the face of U.S. dominance. China guards its sovereignty no less than does Russia, but, as Lo writes,

China, contrary to Russia, "does not deem it necessary to contest Western [i.e., American] interests and influence wherever it finds them." Nor does China view Russia as a strategic counterweight to the United States—whereas Russia hopes to use China to balance against the United States. Chinese leaders go out of their way to emphasize that China is still a developing country and that the United States will remain the sole global superpower for a long time to come. It is a concession that leaves them ample room to pursue China's interests, and so they see little point in paying the enormous costs of opposing the United States.

The second main element in China's "peaceful rise" strategy is using Russia for all it is worth—weapons, oil, or acquiescence in China's expanding influence in Central Asia. Under Vladimir Putin, Russia became more practical in its relations with China than it had been under Boris Yeltsin, in the 1990s. Moscow has made sure to trade its support for China's intransigent policies toward Taiwan, Tibet, and Xinjiang for Beijing's endorsement of Russia's heavy-handed approach to combating domestic instability in Chechnya and the North Caucasus. But the deal remains uneven. Moscow's closer ties with Beijing, meanwhile, have not increased its leverage with Washington one iota. By rejecting the role of junior partner to the United States, Russia has, perhaps unintentionally, become China's junior partner—an arrangement, furthermore, that will last only as long as it is convenient for Beijing. Lo concludes, "China's rise as the next global superpower threatens Russia, not with the military or demographic invasion many fear, but with progressive displacement to the periphery of international decision making."

One should not forget China's many vulnerabilities, nor Russia's numerous foreign policy achievements over the last decade. After the abject humiliation of the 1990s, the sovereignty of the Russian state has been restored—no longer can foreign capitals dictate Russian policy or the appointments of government officials. Russia's annual GDP has soared from a low of $200 billion under Yeltsin to around $1.6 trillion today (a turnabout in which China's insatiable demand for global commodities and manufactures has played an enormous role). Russia enjoys strong relations with France, Germany, and Italy and cultivates these bilateral ties in Europe in order to blunt the collective power of the EU. Its European partners compete with one another for Moscow's favor. At the same time, Russia has—from its point of view at least—demonstrated anew its influence in the former Soviet republics.

But despite its revival, Russia, in contrast to China, remains unable to figure out how to benefit from the immovable fact of U.S. power and wealth. Under the Obama administration, the United States has stopped—for the time being—approaching Russia as a state to be reformed or disciplined. But a softening in tone cannot make up for the fact that the U.S.-Russian relationship lacks the kind of deep commercial basis that undergirds U.S.-Chinese ties. Although an interest in both Russia and the United States in renewed arms control negotiations may help restart bilateral relations, such gestures are no substitute for the kind of economic interdependence Washington has with Beijing.

The ultimate stumbling block between Russia and the United States—and what differentiates China from Russia from the United States' perspective—is the clash over influence in the former Soviet republics. Two factors have led to this clash. The first is that Moscow has lost its empire yet will not relinquish its assertion of "privileged interests" in Georgia, Ukraine, and the other former Soviet republics. Russia's influence in the former Soviet territories—which remained strong even during Russia's perceived weakness in the 1990s—has only grown. This reality, moreover, is an outgrowth not of military occupation or of Russia's clumsy bullying but of mutual interests forged through economic ties.

The second factor is that the United States will not cease to view these lands in terms of promoting or defending democracy, even under the Obama administration's more pragmatic foreign policy. Compare, for example, the relatively small role Tibet plays in U.S.-Chinese relations with the disproportionate hold that now-independent countries such as Georgia or Ukraine have on U.S.-Russian relations. For Washington to appear to abandon the nominal democracies living in Russia's shadow for the sake of more constructive relations with Russia is politically impossible. No matter how badly those countries misgovern themselves or provoke Russia, a withdrawal of U.S. support would be an abandonment of one of the central tenets of U.S. policy toward the region since the end of the Cold War.

The upshot is that Russia and the United States are left with something of a paradox. Although Washington can refuse to defer to Russia's claim of "privileged interests" in the former Soviet states, it cannot undo the fact that such a Russian sphere of influence does exist, extending to property ownership, business and intelligence ties, television programming, and the Internet. Moscow, meanwhile, cannot hope to both claim its interests in its neighbors and emulate China's approach of accepting the role of junior partner to the United States for practical benefit.

This suggests that "the new geopolitics" Lo promises to illuminate are not so new, after all. As Russia pursues the chimera of a multipolar world, the United States pursues the delusion of nearly limitless NATO expansion. And in the process, both unwittingly conspire to put Russia in China's pocket.

THE TRIANGLE TIPS OVER

Lo's book inspires three broad observations. First, although Russia has been known as the world power that straddles Asia and Europe, today it is China that has emerged as the force to be reckoned with on both continents. Russia's Pacific coast serves not as a gateway to Asia—as San Francisco and Los Angeles do in the United States—but as a natural geographic limit. At the same time, China, as the dominant power in East Asia, denies Russia a significant say in the region.

Russia's failure to become an East Asian power over the past several centuries is amplified by emigration from Russia's Far East, where the population has shrunk from a peak of around ten million in the Soviet period to around 6.5 million today. Meanwhile, the population of China's three northeastern provinces directly across the Russian border is estimated at 108 million and growing. As Dmitry Rogozin, now Russia's ambassador to NATO, quipped on Russian radio in 2005, the Chinese are crossing the border "in small groups of five million." Actually, as Lo indicates, the number of Chinese residents in Russia—mostly laborers and petty traders—is probably only between 200,000 and 400,000. Yet Rogozin's quote reflects domestic anxieties about Russia's weak footprint in Asia, a problem for which Russia has no discernible strategy. And on Russia's western border, China's relations with Europe are at least good as Russia's. In other words, Russia's bluff of maintaining an influential presence in Asia is becoming an ever more pronounced strategic weakness.

Second, not only has China shifted its strategic alliance from the Soviet Union to the United States; it has learned how to have its cake and eat it, too. China manages to preserve relations with its Cold War patron, Russia, while hitching its growth to the world's current hegemon, the United States. From 1949 until the Sino-Soviet split in the 1960s, China was an eager junior partner to the Soviet Union, slavishly imitating the Stalinist developmental model. In 1972, the courting of Mao Zedong by Richard Nixon and Henry Kissinger opened up a global option for China that Mao's successors would later exploit. Under Deng Xiaoping, who in 1979 became the first

Chinese Communist leader to visit the United States, China began to forge its de facto strategic alliance with the United States. Then, under Jiang Zemin, a post-1991 rapprochement with Russia became a major additional instrument for Beijing. It is as if China went to the prom with one partner, Russia, went home with another, the United States, and then married the latter while wooing its jilted original date as a mistress.

Third, although the Soviet Union ultimately capitulated to the United States in the Cold War, Russia today does not feel compelled to similarly bow down to the United States. Such a proud stance may not offer many rewards for Russia, but it does confront the United States with some difficult policy questions. Simply put, if Moscow's fantasy is multipolarity, Washington's own delusion has been the near-limitless expansion of NATO. That game, however, is exhausted. For years, the cogent argument against continued NATO expansion was not that it would anger the Russians—after the Soviet collapse, the Russians were going to emerge angry regardless. Rather, the problem was that the bigger NATO became, the weaker it got. Poland agreed to install Patriot missile interceptors—a U.S. and not a NATO missile defense system—only because the United States provided Poland, a member of NATO, with a security guarantee above and beyond that offered by the NATO charter. What, then, is NATO for? Russia will never join, and for all its historic achievements, NATO is not up to solving the contemporary security dilemmas of Europe, such as those linked to energy, migration, and terrorism.

Russia has recovered from its moment of post-Soviet weakness but nonetheless remains a regional power that acts like a global superpower. China, on the other hand, has been transformed into a global superpower but still mostly acts like a regional power. Meanwhile, the United States is still busy trying to consolidate its triumph in the Cold War 18 years on. Recently, many people in Russia and the United States have begun to speak of a "new Cold War." This idea, however, is doubly wrong—wrong because Russia, a regional power, cannot hope to mount a global challenge to the United States, and wrong because the old Cold War tilting never went away, with the battleground merely having been downsized, shifting from the whole globe to Kiev and Tbilisi.

There are domestic advantages for the Russian regime in continuing to talk of a new Cold War. But what does a preoccupation with the supposed Russian menace do for the United States? And alternatively, what would the United States gain from resetting U.S.-Russian relations? At the moment, the most important U.S. policy questions are domestic, not foreign, and Russia will be of little help in solving them. Russia has no role to play in reforming the U.S. health-care system—whose cost structure is the single greatest threat to U.S. power and prosperity—nor can it help fix the crumbling U.S. retirement system. If the United States were to imitate China and indulge Russia in its fantasy about its own global relevance, it would not realize the same kind of concrete benefits the Chinese get. On the international front, although many in Washington see Moscow as Tehran's main backer—even though China has deeper commercial ties to Iran—Russia does not have the leverage over Iran to forestall the development of that country's nuclear weapons program.

The overall importance of Russia for the United States, then, is widely exaggerated. There is one crucial exception, however, an area in which Russia's power has not depreciated: in Europe, Russia remains a dominant force, and its strategic weight in the region is reason alone for the United States to pursue better bilateral relations. During the Crimean War of 1853–56, Lord Palmerston, the British prime minister, fantasized that "the best and most effectual security for the future peace of Europe would be the severance from Russia of some of the frontier territories acquired by her in later times, Georgia,

Circassia, the Crimea, Bessarabia, Poland and Finland. . . . She would still remain an enormous power, but far less advantageously posted for aggression on her neighbors." This flight of imagination has since become reality, and then some. But still, Russia remains a regional force. Indulging the claims that Russia's recent revival is solely attributable to oil—a code word for "luck"—or that Russia's demographic problems will make the country essentially vanish cannot alter the fact that enduring security in Europe cannot be had without Russia's cooperation or in opposition to Russia. An expanded NATO, meanwhile, is not providing the enduring security it once promised. It is only a matter of time before a crisis, perhaps on the territory of a former Soviet republic and now NATO member, exposes NATO's mutual defense pact as wholly inoperative.

There is another reason the United States should care about Russia: because China does. As Lo writes, "China will become steadily (if cautiously) more assertive, initially in East Asia and Central Asia, but eventually across much of Eurasia." In other words, even under a strategy of a peaceful rise, China will increasingly force the United States to accommodate Chinese power. China's development of a blue-water navy recalls the rise of the German navy in the years before World War I, a process that unnerved the United Kingdom, then the world's great power. It seems that China is already trying to recalibrate the balance of power in East Asia, as evidenced by its harassment of the *Impeccable*, a U.S. Navy surveillance ship, in the South China Sea in March 2009. In the event of a crisis, China does not want its thoroughly globalized economy to be vulnerable to a blockade by either the Japanese navy or the U.S. Navy, and it likely envisions being able to hinder U.S. access to the Taiwan Strait. Meanwhile, China is counting on the Russian navy's not rising again in East Asia and on continued strained ties between Japan and Russia over the disputed Kuril Islands, a few rocks in the Pacific Ocean.

In the end, there can be no resetting of U.S.-Russian relations without a transcending of NATO and the establishment of a new security architecture in Europe. And without such a genuine reset, China will retain the upper hand, not only in its bilateral relationship with Russia but also in the strategic triangle comprising China, Russia, and the United States.

Not So Dire Straits

How the Finlandization of Taiwan Benefits U.S. Security

Bruce Gilley

JANUARY/FEBRUARY 2010

Since 2005, Taiwan and China have been moving into a closer economic and political embrace—a process that accelerated with the election of the pro-détente politician Ma Ying-jeou as Taiwan's president in 2008. This strengthening of relations presents the United States with its greatest challenge in the Taiwan Strait since 1979, when Washington severed ties with Taipei and established diplomatic relations with Beijing.

In many ways, the current thaw serves Taipei's interests, but it also allows Beijing to assert increasing influence over Taiwan. As a consensus emerges in Taiwan on establishing closer relations with China, the thaw is calling into question the United States' deeply ambiguous policy, which is supposed to serve both Taiwan's interests (by allowing it to retain its autonomy) and the United States' own (by guarding against an expansionist China). Washington now faces a stark choice: continue

BRUCE GILLEY is Assistant Professor of Political Science at Portland State University's Mark O. Hatfield School of Government and the author of *The Right to Rule: How States Win and Lose Legitimacy*. For an annotated guide to this topic, see "What to Read on Taiwanese Politics" at www.foreignaffairs.com/readinglists/taiwan.

pursuing a militarized realist approach—using Taiwan to balance the power of a rising China—or follow an alternative liberal logic that seeks to promote long-term peace through closer economic, social, and political ties between Taiwan and China.

A TALE OF TWO DÉTENTES

After the Chinese Civil War ended in 1949, Taiwan and mainland China became separate political entities, led, respectively, by Chiang Kai-shek's defeated nationalist party, the Kuomintang (KMT), and Mao Zedong's victorious Chinese Communist Party (CCP). For nearly three decades, Chiang and Mao harbored rival claims to the whole territory of China. Gradually, most of the international community came to accept Beijing's claims to territorial sovereignty over Taiwan and a special role in its foreign relations. By 1972, when U.S. President Richard Nixon visited China, 69 percent of the United Nations' member states had already severed diplomatic ties with Taiwan in favor of relations with China.

The United States, which had merely "acknowledged" Beijing's claim to Taiwan, was slow to recognize the People's Republic of China due to Washington's historical ties with the KMT, dating back to World War II and its conflict with the PRC during the Korean War. The strategic position of Taiwan, astride western Pacific sea and air lanes, gave it added importance. But by 1979, even Washington had recognized Beijing. That same year, the United States enacted the Taiwan Relations Act in order to ensure continued legal, commercial, and de facto diplomatic relations with the island. At the last minute, Senate Republicans—along with several Democrats who worried that President Jimmy Carter was disregarding Taiwan's security—amended the legislation to include promises of arms sales to Taipei and a broader U.S. commitment to "resist any resort to force or other forms of coercion" against the island.

The fading of the Chiang-Mao rivalry, which subsided after both leaders died in the mid-1970s, coupled with Beijing's new inward-looking focus on economic development, made these military commitments appear anachronistic during the 1980s. Beijing ended its shelling of the Taiwanese islands off the Chinese coast and welcomed Taiwanese "compatriots" to the mainland for tourism, investment, and family reunification. Taiwan's native-born president, Lee Teng-hui, who came to power in 1988, had no interest in "retaking the mainland" and approved the creation of such exchanges. In 1993, the heads of the two governments' cross-strait contact groups held their first direct talks, in Singapore.

This "first détente" ended abruptly in 1995, when the United States issued a visa for Lee to visit Cornell University. China, in the midst of a domestic leadership transition, was already hardening its position on Taiwan, and armchair generals in all three places were publishing books on the predicted order of battle to come. Beijing saw the visa as a betrayal of earlier U.S. promises to refrain from any official relations with Taiwanese leaders. Taiwan's democratization was also leading to domestic popular pressures for a more assertive stance on independence. Beijing reacted by hurling missiles into the Taiwan Strait in 1995 and 1996. Washington dispatched aircraft carriers and radar ships to the area. Beijing's worst fears were then realized in 2000, when Taiwanese citizens elected Chen Shui-bian as their president. Chen, the leader of the Democratic Progressive Party (DPP), now the opposition, promised to seek formal recognition of Taiwan's de facto independence from China. As a consequence, cross-strait relations deteriorated dramatically between 1995 and 2005, leading to a renewed emphasis on militarization by all three sides.

The damage wrought by this "second freeze" led to serious rethinking in all three capitals. Beijing worried that its aggressive posture on Taiwan was threatening its broader influence in

Asia, as other nations rallied behind the U.S. security shield; Taipei began to reevaluate the value of its symbolic assertions of nationhood; and Washington began to question its unlimited commitment to an increasingly troublesome Taiwan, which threatened to damage, if not destroy, its more important relationship with China. By the end of George W. Bush's first term, Washington had become the main check on Taipei's assertions of independence.

The "second détente" in cross-strait relations began with a 2005 speech by Chinese President Hu Jintao downplaying demands for reunification. Beijing was shifting its view as a result of an emerging grand strategy that stressed regional and global influence; accordingly, it came to see Taiwan less as an ideologically charged and urgent matter and more as a pragmatic and low-key management issue. Ma's election in 2008 signaled the resurgence of a similar vision in Taiwan. He promised "no unification, no independence, no use of force." Within months, in rapid and unprecedented fashion, the heads of the contact groups began holding semiannual meetings and signed more than two dozen previously unthinkable agreements. Although most of these involved economic matters, they had political implications, too. The number of Chinese tourists visiting Taiwan—including Taiwan's long-militarized islands directly off the coast of China—surged by a factor of ten, to 3,000 per day. China sent students to Taiwan, and the two sides authorized 270 flights per week across the strait. Important political fears that had previously restricted economic integration suddenly dissipated on both sides, and Taipei and Beijing began talking about the "total normalization" of their economic and financial ties. The supposedly fixed national interests on which foreign policy realists base their assessments were in total flux.

The second détente has also included explicitly political deals. China had previously permitted Taiwan to participate only in international organizations with an economic focus, such as the Asian Development Bank, the Asia-Pacific Economic Cooperation (APEC), and the World Trade Organization. In 2009, it allowed Taiwan to participate as an observer at the annual board meeting of the World Health Organization (WHO) in Geneva. Both sides began discussing a Taiwanese presence in the UN bodies responsible for civil aviation, commercial shipping, meteorology, and climate change.

Both sides also tacitly agreed to a "diplomatic truce": Beijing ceased courting the nations on Taiwan's dwindling list of 23 diplomatic allies, and in 2009 Taipei dropped its perpetual request for UN membership for the first time in 17 years. When Ma was reelected as KMT chair in July 2009, Hu declared that he would like to build "mutual trust between the two sides in political affairs." As political relations warmed, Taiwanese officials—including leading DPP figures, such as the mayor of Kaohsiung—became regular visitors in China.

There are indications that this second cross-straits détente will last. Although both leaders' terms will expire in 2012, Hu's designated successor, Xi Jinping, is a well-known advocate of cross-strait exchanges. Ma, meanwhile, has recovered from the political damage wrought by Typhoon Morakot, which struck the island in August 2009. So long as the DPP remains divided between extreme anti-détente and limited-détente factions, he seems likely to win reelection.

Taiwan and China are now approaching their relationship using completely different assumptions than those that governed cross-strait relations for decades. Whereas they previously saw the relationship as a military dispute, today both sides have embraced a view of security that is premised on high-level contact, trust, and reduced threats of force. Their views of economic issues, meanwhile, have placed global integration and competitiveness ahead of nationalist protectionism. This represents a fundamental shift in the political relationship between Taiwan and China.

Not So Dire Straits

FROM HELSINKI TO TAIPEI

To understand the evolution of the Taipei-Beijing relationship, it is useful to consider the theory and practice of what has become known as "Finlandization" in the field of political science. The term derives its name from Finland's 1948 agreement with the Soviet Union under which Helsinki agreed not to join alliances challenging Moscow or serve as a base for any country challenging Soviet interests. In return, the Kremlin agreed to uphold Finnish autonomy and respect Finland's democratic system. Therefore, from 1956 to 1981, under the leadership of President Urho Kekkonen, Finland pursued a policy of strategic appeasement and neutrality on U.S.-Soviet issues and limited domestic criticism of the Soviet Union. This policy enjoyed wide support in Finland at the time (despite the subsequent debate in Finland on its merits). Kekkonen also won praise across the political spectrum in the United States, especially from foreign policy realists such as George Kennan, who lauded the Finnish leader's "composure and firmness."

Building on the work of others, the Danish political scientist Hans Mouritzen in 1988 proposed a general theory of Finlandization known as "adaptive politics." Mouritzen stressed the fundamental difference between a Finlandized regime and a client, or "puppet," state, explaining that the former makes some concessions to a larger neighbor in order to guarantee important elements of its independence—voluntary choices that the latter could never make. Unlike a puppet regime, a Finlandized state calculates that its long-term interests, and perhaps those of its neighbors, are best served by making strategic concessions to a superpower next door. These concessions are motivated chiefly by geographic proximity, psychological threats from the superpower, and cultural affinities between the two sides. Being so close, the superpower need only issue vague threats, rather than display actual military muscle, to change its weaker neighbor's policies. Meanwhile, the small power perceives itself as engaging in an "active and principled neutrality," rather than a cowering acquiescence, a distinction that is critical to rationalizing these policy changes domestically.

Finlandization posed a direct challenge to the dominant realist logic of the Cold War, which held that concessions to Soviet power were likely to feed Moscow's appetite for expansion. Even if one rejects the theory of Finlandization, it is difficult to deny that Kekkonen played a constructive role in ending the Cold War. In 1969, for instance, Finland offered itself as the venue for a conference between the two blocs that eventually produced a shared document with clear commitments to human rights and freedoms: the Helsinki accords.

Cold War historians, such as John Lewis Gaddis, believe that the Helsinki process was central to undermining the moral authority of the Soviet Union, and others have argued that it prompted the ideological shift necessary to kickstart Mikhail Gorbachev's perestroika in the mid-1980s. Moreover, Finland's unique status as interlocutor with Moscow made possible the first serious discussions of nuclear disarmament and of the shared development of Arctic resources, both of which served as templates for the warming of relations between NATO and the Soviet bloc. Although it usually has a negative connotation, "Finlandization" need not be a pejorative term.

Taiwan shares many of the key features that characterized Finland in the late 1940s. It is a small but internally sovereign state that is geographically close to a superpower with which it shares cultural and historical ties. Its fierce sense of independence is balanced by a pragmatic sense of the need to accommodate that superpower's vital interests. Most important, the evolving views of its leaders and its people today focus on seeking security through integration rather than confrontation. This approach could help defuse one of the most worrying trends in global politics: the emerging rivalry between China and the United States.

The analogy is not perfect. U.S. security guarantees for Taiwan today are more explicit than they were for Finland during the Cold War, although few doubt that NATO would have defended Finland against a Soviet invasion. And China's 1,000-plus missiles targeted at Taiwan are a more direct threat than anything the Soviet military ever mustered across the Vuoksi River. But in general the thinking that has motivated the second détente on both sides parallels that which led to the Finnish-Soviet détente of the Cold War. Although it is still early, Taipei is moving in the direction of eventual Finlandization.

Under such a scenario, Taiwan would reposition itself as a neutral power, rather than a U.S. strategic ally, in order to mollify Beijing's fears about the island's becoming an obstacle to China's military and commercial ambitions in the region. It would also refrain from undermining the CCP's rule in China. In return, Beijing would back down on its military threats, grant Taipei expanded participation in international organizations, and extend the island favorable economic and social benefits.

The DPP's director of international affairs, Hsiao Bi-khim, has written that the changes in Taiwan's China policy "are leading to a new strategic outlook, which aligns Taiwan with China's sphere of influence instead of maintaining the traditional presumed informal alliance with the United States." Although Hsiao, like many in the DPP, fears this sort of shift, such reservations are unwarranted.

A MEANS OR AN END?

There are two ways to view the shift in Chinese policy toward Taiwan. The dominant interpretation has long been that Beijing is motivated by nationalism and that the PRC's irredentist claims to Taiwan stem from a broader national discourse of humiliation and weakness. According to this view, the CCP is striving to reincorporate Taiwan into China in order to avert a domestic nationalist backlash and a crisis of legitimacy. Seen in this light, Taiwan is an end unto itself and the second détente is merely a tactical shift intended to force Taiwan into reunification through indirect means: beneath Beijing's silk glove of détente is the iron fist of nationalism.

In recent years, many Western analysts have rejected this nationalist interpretation of Beijing's Taiwan policy and opted instead for a geostrategic one. Unrecovered territories are legion in the history of the PRC, and the CCP has found it easy to let go of others (including disputed regions bordering Russia, India, and the Spratly Islands, as well as control over Mongolia and Korea). Taiwan, however, by virtue of its geographic location, represents a potential strategic threat to China. It could serve as a base for foreign military operations against China and even in peacetime could constrain Beijing's ability to develop and project naval power and ensure maritime security in East Asia.

Beijing's core goal from this perspective is the preservation of its dominance in its immediate offshore region, as became clear in 2009 when five Chinese vessels trailed a U.S. Navy ship sailing near a Chinese submarine base. Taiwan represents an obstacle to this goal if it remains a U.S. strategic ally armed with advanced U.S. weaponry, but not if it becomes a self-defending and neutral state with close economic and political ties to China. Beijing's constantly changing position on Taiwan—which has incrementally moderated from "liberation" to "peaceful unification" to "one China" to "anti-independence" since Mao's era—in fact reflects a concern with Taiwan's geostrategic status, not with the precise nature of its political ties to China. According to this interpretation, Beijing has no interest in occupying or ruling Taiwan; it simply wants a sphere of influence that increases its global clout and in which Taiwan is a neutral state, not a client state. Seen through this lens, Taiwan is a means to an end and the second détente is a tactic intended to achieve this strategic objective through Taiwan's Finlandization.

China's recent behavior confirms this view; Beijing's decision to allow Taiwan to participate in the WHO represents a cool-headed understanding that giving Taiwan a greater international voice could enhance its independence from the United States, which would, in turn, serve China's own interests. It also gives Beijing an opportunity to show that a China-dominated Asia need not be less peaceful, less prosperous, or even less democratic. As the Chinese scholar Jianwei Wang of the University of Wisconsin–Stevens Point puts it, "Beijing views the Taiwan issue and cross-straits relations as an integral part of China's comprehensive 'rise' in world affairs rather than as an isolated issue purely affecting national pride alone."

Recent survey data lends credence to this argument. The mainland citizens polled by Horizon Research in 2004 were not particularly nationalist about retaking Taiwan—only 15 percent wanted immediate military action, whereas 58 percent believed that the government should rule out the use of force in favor of economic integration. In a 2008 speech, Hu identified "political antagonism," rather than political separation, as the problem in cross-straits relations, breaking with previous pronouncements from Beijing. Subsequent policy statements by the CCP have revealed a calm confidence in the shifting geostrategic relationship with Taiwan, not a bombastic nationalist urgency for reunification.

THE PACIFIER

In 1995, at the end of the first détente, Chen-shen Yen, a Taiwanese scholar and KMT adviser, wrote a paper in the Taiwanese political journal *Wenti yu Yanjiu* explicitly extolling the logic of Finlandization (or *fenlanhua* in Chinese) for

Taiwan. By seeking Beijing's approval for an expanded international voice, maintaining a foreign policy that did not threaten China, and choosing leaders who enjoyed Beijing's trust, Yen argued, Taiwan could do more to protect its internal autonomy and economic prosperity than it could by challenging the rising superpower on its doorstep. Moreover, Taiwan's long-term interests in gaining true independence could only be achieved by democratization in China, which would be more likely if Taiwan avoided stoking a military or ideological confrontation. His conclusion echoed that of the Athenians in Thucydides' Melian dialogue: "Given the responsibility to protect its future existence," wrote Yen, "a civilized country should adjust itself to external realities." It has taken over a decade for Yen's prescient views to gain currency, but they now have widespread support.

Ma's pursuit of "total normalization" has enjoyed steady and rising popularity in Taiwan since he came to office. It reflects a view that the militarized approach to the cross-strait conflict that has dominated both Taiwanese (and U.S.) strategic thinking since the days of Chiang and Mao has not resolved the dispute and does not serve Taiwan's present needs. Just as Finland, a small country, was able to pioneer a nonmilitarized alternative to the Cold War, so, too, could Taiwan play that role in the brewing U.S.-Chinese cold war in Asia.

At present, a rising China threatens the world primarily because there has been little in the way of domestic political liberalization to keep Beijing's increasing economic and military power in check. Taiwan could play a far greater role in China's liberalization if it were to become a Finlandized part of the region and its officials were able to move across the strait even more freely than they do now. Already, prominent Chinese liberals, such as Zhang Boshu of the Chinese Academy of Social Sciences, are arguing that the mainland should draw lessons about political development from Taiwan. As Sheng

Lijun of the National University of Singapore writes, "With the Taiwan political challenge, Beijing will sooner or later have to improve its governance (including democracy, human rights, and anti-corruption)." Taipei's experience with democratic reform offers many lessons for Beijing—especially because the formerly authoritarian KMT's return to power in 2008 showed that the CCP could one day hope to rule again even if the advent of democracy initially brought another party to power.

Democratic reform in China will be encouraged both by popular pressure to emulate Taiwan (PRC citizens have already enthusiastically adopted Taiwanese pop culture and business practices) and by the brute necessity of managing the relationship in a way that meets the Taiwanese electorate's high expectations of transparency and accountability. Some may call it appeasement, but if Taiwan uses appeasement to democratize and pacify a rising China, it will be a worthy appeasement indeed.

SELLING FINLANDIZATION

Taiwan's continued progress toward Finlandization will depend on whether Ma can demonstrate the tangible benefits of this strategy to the Taiwanese population. He will have to secure an even greater international voice for Taiwan (for example, making its WHO observer status permanent), the ability to negotiate its own free-trade agreements, and the verified removal of some of the more than 1,000 Chinese missiles currently aimed at the island. Best of all would be a peace accord under which China renounced the use of force unless the island were invaded or achieved de jure independence. Such an accord, which both sides are seeking, would be the functional equivalent of the 1948 Soviet-Finnish treaty, allaying the large power's security concerns while assuring the small power of its autonomy. Another potential benefit is a promised economic cooperation framework agreement within which Taiwan could pursue a free-trade agreement with Beijing; Taiwan currently risks becoming uncompetitive in the Chinese market and China-based supply chains as a result of the free-trade agreements between members of the Association of Southeast Asian Nations (ASEAN) and China.

Ma will also have to reassure Taiwanese voters, who fear losing their political freedoms. In Taiwan, there is a justified concern about being lured into a trap of integration with China that would imperil Taiwan's democracy and internal sovereignty (meanwhile, Beijing fears that Taiwan's external sovereignty will grow as its participation in international organizations expands). The University of Wisconsin's Wang, whose analysis reflects the CCP's strategic views, writes ominously that Ma will eventually have to show his goodwill by scaling back Taiwan's arms purchases and acknowledging that reunification is an option in the long term. Wang is correct that Finlandization will not be free of costs for Taiwan. In particular, as was the case in Finland, Taipei will have to restrain anticommunist activism on the island and distance itself from the United States militarily.

Under much domestic pressure and possibly with the tacit consent of Beijing, Ma allowed the Dalai Lama to visit Taiwan in September 2009 to pray for the victims of the typhoon. But the same month he denied entry to the Uighur leader Rebiya Kadeer, citing national security concerns and the public interest. His official statement on the 20th anniversary of the Tiananmen Square massacre—with its delicate reference to a "painful chapter in history" that "must be faced," as similar dark moments in Taiwan's history had to be—was classic Finlandized diplomacy. For Ma, the Tiananmen anniversary was a reminder to "both sides to spur each other to make further improvements in the area of human rights." A similarly tendentious, if ultimately fruitful, moral equivalence on the part of Finnish leaders is what brought the Soviets to Helsinki to talk about human rights.

For now, domestic opposition to Ma's policy is muted. Most controversies on the island concern how to pursue integration with China, not whether to do so. The risks of political dependence on China seem worth it to most Taiwanese, especially given the island's current political dependence on the United States. And Taiwan's youth, in particular, see China as an opportunity rather than a threat. For the DPP to regain power, it will have to embrace this pragmatic consensus on China. The days of the DPP's "just say no" platform on China are over.

Just as Ma must consider the views of the electorate, he must also take into account the reactions of other Asian states. Taiwan could still alienate other Asian nations if it shifted to a more China-centered, Finlandized approach, but this is unlikely because it is exactly what ASEAN has been promoting among its members for ten years or more through its "ASEAN + 3" and ASEAN Regional Forum initiatives. The theory of Finlandization may highlight the uniqueness of Taiwan's situation, but a similar logic already informs policymaking in other Asian capitals. South Korea has been taking a similar tack, and many neighboring nations believe that China can be pacified, as Vietnam was, through inclusion and cooperation. Even Japan, which feels itself to be more vulnerable than other Asian countries to China's rise as a naval power, has an interest in encouraging internal reforms in China and might learn from Taiwan's example. After all, West Germany's successful *Ostpolitik*, which led to a peace treaty with the Soviet Union in 1970, built on the lessons of Finland's accommodation with the Soviet Union.

Far from seeking to alienate other Asian governments, then, the KMT government believes that Taiwan's international status will be enhanced if Taipei falls in step with its neighbors' preferred methods of dealing with a rising China—through accommodation, socialization, and communication.

OUT OF ORBIT

The Finlandization of Taiwan will, of course, pose major challenges to current U.S. policy. An April 2009 Congressional Research Service report recognized this dilemma by asking how Washington ought to react "if Taiwan should continue to move closer to or even align with the PRC." Opinions in Washington are divided between two realist camps. The first wants to allow the changes to proceed so that, in the words of Douglas Paal of the Carnegie Endowment for International Peace, Taiwan does not become a "strategic liability" to the United States. The second wants to rearm Taiwan so that, in the words of Dennis Blair, the U.S. national intelligence director, Taiwan is not "so defenseless that it feels that it has to do everything that China says." Neither camp seems to accept, much less endorse, the liberal logic of Finlandization as an alternative security strategy for Taiwan.

Taiwan has played a strategic role in U.S. foreign policy since the 1940s—first it served as a buffer against communist expansion out of North Korea, and more recently it has been a bulwark against a rising China. It is strategically located along East Asian shipping lanes and could provide another naval resupply site if China continues to limit U.S. naval visits to Hong Kong. Keeping Taiwan within the U.S. orbit has served Washington's interests by demonstrating that the United States will continue to engage in Asia, despite talk of a declining U.S. role in the region. The tragic result of this policy, however, has been that it has played into Beijing's fears of encirclement and naval inferiority, which in turn has prompted China's own military buildup.

Finlandization will allow Taiwan to break this cycle by taking itself out of the game and moderating the security dilemma that haunts the Washington-Beijing relationship. The cross-strait freeze of 1995–2005 raised fears in Washington that

Taiwan was becoming a strategic liability for the United States. Ma's policies have momentarily resolved that concern. And if the United States uses the current opportunity to adjust its own policies and support the détente, that concern could be rendered moot. This would make future provocations by either side less likely.

Taipei's decision to chart a new course is a godsend for a U.S. administration that increasingly needs China's cooperation in achieving its highest priority: maintaining the peaceful international liberal order. The United States requires Beijing's support on a host of pressing world issues—from climate change to financial stability and nuclear nonproliferation. William Stanton, Washington's de facto ambassador to Taiwan, admitted as much in October 2009, declaring that "it's in everybody's interests, including Taiwan's as well, that the U.S. try to have a cooperative relationship with China."

In recent years, the U.S.-Taiwanese relationship has been increasingly dictated by the interests of narrow lobbies rather than grand strategy. The U.S. arms industry, the Taiwanese military, and Taiwanese independence activists together make a formidable force. Before the current détente, Taiwan's staunch anticommunism and adversarial policy toward China aligned well with Washington's own ideology and militarized approach to the Taiwan Strait. But the recent evolution of tactical and strategic thinking in Taipei and Beijing has created a disjuncture. The adversarial status quo that the United States has protected is no longer the status quo that the Taiwanese want protected.

Obviously, if Ma were to compromise Taiwan's democratic institutions in pursuit of détente with China, Washington would have reason to complain. But if a democratic Taiwan continues to move into China's orbit, Washington should follow the lead of the Taiwanese people in redefining their future. In the past, U.S. "noninterference" meant maintaining the balance of power across the strait and challenging Beijing's provocations. Today, it means reducing the militarization of the conflict and not interfering with Taiwan's Finlandization.

Even from a strictly realist perspective, there is no need for the United States to keep Taiwan within its strategic orbit, given that U.S. military security can be attained through other Asian bases and operations. Taiwan's Finlandization should be seen not as a necessary sacrifice to a rising China but rather as an alternative strategy for pacifying China. Washington should drop its zero-sum view of the Taipei-Beijing relationship and embrace the strategic logic underlying the rapprochement—in effect "losing China" a second time by allowing Taiwan to drift into the PRC's sphere of influence.

Ma told a visiting congressional delegation in August 2009 that his détente would be "beneficial to all parties concerned." He is right. As was the case with Finland and the Soviet Union, Taiwan has an inherent interest in a peaceful and democratic China. Washington needs to embrace this shift not only because it serves its own long-term strategic aims in Asia and globally but also because what the Taiwanese people choose to do with their sovereign democratic power is up to them. The overburdened giant should happily watch from a distance and focus on other pressing regional and global issues.

SIDELINING UNCLE SAM

The United States has played a crucial role in maintaining cross-strait peace and encouraging democracy in Taiwan since 1949. Today, the U.S. role in this process is nearing its end. U.S. policy toward a Finlandized Taiwan will have to be adjusted both strategically and diplomatically. Expanded official contacts with Taiwan will require consultations with Beijing; the United States and its allies will have to refashion battle plans to exclude Taiwan; Washington will have to support the new approach to cross-strait peace through its public diplomacy; and U.S. intelligence agencies will have to be more careful about scrutinizing technology transfers to the island because the PRC's intelligence gathering on Taiwan will inevitably expand. Most important, Washington will have to significantly scale back its arms sales to Taipei.

In 1982, the United States pledged to China that it would reduce its arms sales to Taiwan—a promise that it has conspicuously broken ever since. Today, as then, there is a golden opportunity to demilitarize the conflict. The U.S. Congress is not particularly interested in pressing President Barack Obama on the issue, and Taiwan's economic decline has moderated Taipei's appetite for major arms purchases anyway. In the past, sales of fighter jets, destroyers, tanks, and missiles to Taiwan were premised as much on the political message they sent to Beijing as on their tactical value. In the new climate, Washington can reinforce the détente by holding back planned sales of items such as Black Hawk helicopters, Patriot missiles, and additional fighter jets. The Pentagon must view the shift not as simply a minor adjustment due to reduced cross-strait tensions but as a wholesale rejection of the vision of Taiwan as a militarized base within the U.S. strategic orbit.

By signaling that Washington is finally respecting China's territorial integrity, these reductions could, in turn, lead to verifiable force reductions by China, as well as to an end to its Taiwan-focused military attack drills. Removing Taiwan as a major player in the United States' Asian security strategy would have ripple effects on U.S. strategy in the region as a whole. Indeed, it is likely that Asian-only security organizations, such as the ASEAN Regional Forum, would increasingly take the lead in defining Asia's future security architecture.

The arguments in favor of Finlandization are stronger today than ever before: a Finlandized Taiwan would play a much more transformative role in China itself, thus improving the chances of a peacefully rising China. As was the case for Finland in its relations with the Soviet Union, Taiwan could create a model for the peaceful resolution of China's many resource, boundary, and military conflicts throughout Asia. More broadly, the Taiwan-China détente is a test of liberal approaches to international relations—specifically, the notion that a broad integration of domestic interests will pacify relations between states far more than a militarized balance of power.

Taiwan has always been a frontline state in the rivalry between Washington and Beijing. In the past, that meant the United States' fending off China's plans to invade Taiwan and defying Beijing's opposition to the island's democratic development. Today, with Taiwan's territory secure and democracy consolidated, Taiwan's role on the frontlines is changing again. It is now Washington's turn to confront and adapt to this historic shift.

CPSIA information can be obtained at www.ICGtesting.com
Printed in the USA
LVOW012150170112

264360LV00007B/192/P